Wiccan Crystals

Wiccan Crystals

Harness the power of magical stones for spells, rituals, and more

Cerridwen Greenleaf

CICO BOOKS
LONDON NEW YORK

Published in 2024 by CICO Books
An imprint of Ryland Peters & Small Ltd
20–21 Jockey's Fields   341 E 116th St
London WC1R 4BW   New York, NY 10029

www.rylandpeters.com

10 9 8 7 6 5 4 3 2 1

Text in this book originally featured in *The Magical Home, 5-Minute Magic for Modern Wiccans, Spells for Peace of Mind, The Book of Witchy Wellbeing, The Book of Norse Magic, Wiccan Moon Magic,* and *Magic for Change*

A CIP catalog record for this book is available from the Library of Congress and the British Library.

ISBN: 978-1-80065-370-2

Printed in China

Illustrator: Nina Hunter
Assistant editor: Danielle Rawlings
Commissioning editor: Kristine Pidkameny
Senior designer: Emily Breen
Art director: Sally Powell
Creative director: Leslie Harrington
Production manager: Gordana Simakovic
Publishing manager: Carmel Edmonds

Safety note: Please note that while the use of essential oils, herbs, incense, and particular practices refer to healing benefits, they are not intended to replace diagnosis of illness or ailments, or healing or medicine. Always consult your doctor or other health professional in the case of illness, pregnancy, and personal sensitivities and conditions. Neither the author nor the publisher can be held responsible for any claim arising out of the general information, recipes, and practices provided in the book.

Contents

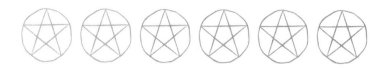

Introduction

Gems are powerful tools that can pave the way for a better life for you. There is a long history of the use of gems, stones, and crystals as amulets, symbols, charms, and jewelry in magic. These myriad stones can really enrich your life in so many ways. Do you want to get a new job? Jade jewelry magic will do the trick! Need to get over a heartbreak? A chrysocolla heart-healing spell will soothe your soul. Are you an author suffering from the dreaded writer's block? A creativity crystal incantation is exactly what you need.

If you are a beginner at witchcraft, they might seem a bit bewildering and whimsical to you, especially if you have seen complex crystal grids or the massive crystal collections amassed by other witches. That may well be your end goal, but you need not feel overwhelmed by the startling number of different crystals and their properties or the never-ending possibilities of crystal magic. At its heart, crystal magic is quite simple.

Crystals each have unique vibrational energies, which you can use to connect yourself to the Earth and are associated with a vast spectrum of healing properties. One of the fundamentals of crystal magic is intention—a crystal can be programmed with your intentions and desires and will in turn magnify your intent and assist you in bringing forth whatever sorts of changes or benefits you are seeking. It is always best to do your research and find crystals whose inherent properties complement the intention you want to focus on.

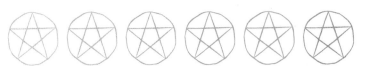

With crystal magic, you will learn to improve your life in ways large and small. You will discover the stones that are special to you and how to fully utilize birthstones and karmic crystals. You will undertake the magical arts of crystal conjuring and spell casting with stones. You will be inducted into the practice of healing with crystals and how to achieve wellness every day. Crystals are not only a beautiful product of nature that are great for jewelry and decoration, but they are also filled with positive energy and have been used for healing and magic across the globe for centuries. Incorporating them into rituals adds a fresh layer of mysticism to your life that will guide you to an even deeper connection with your spirituality and also be a great benefit to your mental health.

Yes, through the magic of gems, anything is possible. Again, welcome to this glittering and magical realm—I hope you're ready to begin a special journey under a sky where every star is a jewel you can wish upon!

CHAPTER 1

Crystal Basics and Getting Started

The Magic of Crystals

We have a vast healing and life-enhancing trove of beautiful and sacred stones from which to choose, and each stone has its own inherent, divine qualities. Each one is unique for the energy it emits and how it interacts with our subtle energy field, or aura. In the same way that no two fingerprints or snowflakes are alike, each crystal is completely individual, never to be repeated again in nature.

Crystals found in nature are imbued with special qualities from the minerals and rocks surrounding them. Geologists are fond of explaining the varying colors of crystals as chemical impurities.

I prefer to liken the development of crystalline color to the making of a fine wine, whereby the soil and even the neighboring trees, plants, sun, and rain affect the grapes and the resulting nectar. Gems, too, have notes, like a perfume or a wine or even music.

The use of gems and crystals in rituals, spells, and affirmations has been part of the human experience for millennia. By incorporating this practice into your life, you will create a flow of positive energy that will enable you to enhance your work, your family, your love, and every other part of your existence.

CRYSTAL BENEFITS

Inspiration: Amazonite, aventurine, carnelian, chrysolite, chrysoprase, citrine, green tourmaline, malachite, yellow fluorite

Intuition: amethyst, azurite, celestite, lapis lazuli, moonstone, selenite, smoky quartz, sodalite, star sapphire, yellow calcite

Love: amethyst, magnetite, rhodochrosite, rose quartz, twinned rock crystals

Abundance: bloodstone, carnelian, citrine, dendritic agate, diamond, garnet, hawk's eye, moss agate, peridot, ruby, tiger's eye, topaz, yellow sapphire

Protection: amber, Apache tear, chalcedony, citrine, green calcite, jade, jet, smoky quartz

Self-belief: azurite, chalcedony, chrysocolla, green tourmaline, rutilated quartz, tiger's eye

Serenity: amber, aventurine, blue jade, dioptase, Herkimer diamond, jasper, kunzite, moonstone, onyx, peridot, quartz, rhodonite

Confidence: carnelian, obsidian, quartz, selenite, sodalite, topaz

Positive energy: agate, aventurine, bloodstone, calcite, chalcedony, citrine, dioptase, emerald, garnet, orange calcite, ruby, topaz

Deep wisdom: emerald, fluorite, Herkimer diamond, moldavite, serpentine, yellow calcite

Crystal Cleansing Salt Spell

The first thing you need to do when you get a new crystal is to cleanse it, so it does not shed any potentially negative vibrations from others.

GATHER TOGETHER

1 cup (200 g) sea salt

glass bowl

crystal to be cleansed

black candle

sage bundle

fireproof dish

Add the salt to the glass bowl and put your crystal on top of the salt. Light the black candle, then light the sage from the candle flame and put it in the fireproof dish. Speak this spell:

Bone of the earth, filled with ancient power,

Filled with grounding, filled with healing.

Let go of all that came before.

You are now here. You are welcome here.

With harm to none, and blessings to all.

Roll the crystal so every side touches the salt and then repeat the spell. Snuff both the sage and the candle and let the stone rest in the salt overnight. In the morning, remove the crystal and let it power up on your altar to become imbued with your energy and magical intention. Take the salt out of your home and dispose of it at least a block away. Your stone is now ready to serve your needs.

ANCIENT POWER

The earliest humans made use of the unique properties of crystals. For example, amber, one of my absolute favorite gems, was probably the first stone used as ornamentation, when people of the Stone Age discovered rock-hard resin deposits. Roughly rounded beads were used for necklaces, belts, and pouches. Archeologists and anthropologists have found many sites in which precious amber was buried with the tools and remains of shamans, medicine men, and rulers. Since the beginning of mankind, this stone has been thought to have healing properties, a belief that stays with us to this day. But the Egyptians were perhaps the people most conscious of the power of crystals, using them even in the cornerstones of the Great Pyramids. They used gems as objects of protection, power, wisdom, and love for both the living and the dead. Secret knowledge of these sacred stones and their magical properties has been passed down to us and it has been embraced very enthusiastically. This is wonderful as it is one more way Mother Earth offers her healing energy.

Alternatively, to cleanse your crystal, place it in a bowl of sea salt overnight and then leave it in the light of the sun for a day, making sure it is not in direct sunlight so as not to create a fire hazard. You can also surround the crystal with sage leaves, the same kind you would use for smudging (see page 144), and leave them overnight.

Charging Your Crystals

All stones possess natural energies of their very own. You want to merge your energies with those of your crystals so that the crystals will be in sync with your vibratory channel. You can do this by cleansing your crystals (see page 12) and then charging them with your own energy. Remain mindful of the great power your stones have and you will be in a good position to work with it.

Once you've cleansed your crystal, sit in a comfortable position and hold the crystal in your right hand. Focus on the energy you desire your crystal to hold and project it into the stone. Consider carefully what kind of energy you want to place into your crystal. Bear in mind, the use of crystal magic should not be used solely for your purposes, but also for the greater good. Please make sure you're projecting positive energy and not anger or hatred. You should ask aloud for your crystal to work together with you for the highest good. You are doing creative visualization here, so keep concentrating until you can see and feel the energy flowing into the stone. You will feel when the charging, or programming, is complete; your intuition will tell you.

Successful Spellwork

Call forth your powers within to make magic with ritual. Your mind and will are potent magical tools, and ritual is the practice of exercising your will. In order for your spellwork to be successful and a positive force in your life, you need to think a few things through.

First identify your intention, then plan and prepare for your ritual. Once you have gathered your essential ingredients and tools together, and everything is ready, you should relax completely before enacting the ritual. Afterward, clean and clear the space and leave everything in its place.

SETTING YOUR INTENTION

A well-defined and focused intention is the key to success in a life- enhancing ritual. Good results depend upon clarity. If your intention is not crystal clear, you are likely to fail. You must approach your ritual concentrating fully on a definite aim. If a nagging worry is hovering in the back of your mind, you are not properly focused. You may even want to perfect an image of your intention and desire with creative visualization.

Part of your preparation should include using ritual correspondences— the phase of the moon, the day of the week, the color of the candles you use, and much more. These things add to the depth and meaning of your ritual. Do you need to clear the energy and refresh your altar with some housecleaning and smudging? Continue to focus on your intention while doing this; you are creating the foundation for a successful ceremony.

The greater the clarity and concentration you bring to bear, the more powerful your ritual will be.

Lunar and Solar Sign Connections

When the sun or moon is in a certain zodiac sign, it carries that astrological energy. The zodiacal year starts with the sun in Aries, usually on March 21, and the sun then goes through all twelve astrological signs each month. The moon moves more quickly than the sun and stays in a sign for two days before moving on to the next.

You might notice you feel highly energetic one day and more laid back the next. Why is that? Look to the moon for answers. I recommend consulting a reliable source for tracking the sign of the moon. Keep track in your Book of Shadows (see Glossary, page 143) of the effect that these solar and lunar connections have for you. You can further enhance these astrological associations by using the associated crystals and colors for your candles with the energy of these signs—see opposite.

Aries, Mars-ruled sign of the Ram, is a high-energy time, which is good for new beginnings. Associated with diamond, amethyst, topaz, garnet, iron, and steel, and the color red.

Taurus, Venus-ruled sign of the Bull, is very abundant in all ways: money, farming, and love. Associated with coral, sapphire, emerald, turquoise, agate, zircon, and copper, and the color azure.

Gemini is ruled by Mercury and is about smarts, quickness, communication, and travel. Associated with aquamarine, agate, amber, emerald, topaz, and aluminum, and the color electric blue.

Cancer is ruled by the moon and connected with family and home, and is most fertile of all for farming. Associated with opal, pearl, emerald, moonstone, and silver, and the colors pearl and rose.

Leo is ruled by the sun and it is romantic, brave, showy, and a time to lead. Associated with diamond, ruby, gold, sardonyx, and chrysoberyl, and the color orange.

Virgo, Mercury-ruled, is good for health, nutrition, and detailed hard work. Associated with jade, rhodonite, sapphire, carnelian, and aluminum, and the color gray-blue.

Libra is ruled by Venus and is artistic, loving, abundant, and balancing. Associated with opal, sapphire, jade, quartz, turquoise, and copper, and the color pale orange.

Scorpio is Pluto-ruled and very sensual and sexual, bountiful, and a time for strategy. Associated with bloodstone, topaz, aquamarine, jasper, and silver, and the color dark red.

Sagittarius, Jupiter-ruled, connotes philosophy, spirituality, treks, and higher understanding. Associated with lapis lazuli, topaz, turquoise, coral, and tin, and the color purple.

Capricorn is Earth-ruled is good for business, money, jobs, goals, and politics. Associated with onyx, jet, ruby, lead, and malachite, and the color brown.

Aquarius, Uranus-ruled, is a time for intellect, risk, innovation, and interaction. Associated with aquamarine, jade, fluorite, sapphire, zircon, and aluminum, and the color green.

Pisces is ruled by Neptune and is for psychism, dreams, affection, and creativity. Associated with amethyst, alexandrite, bloodstone, stitchite, and silver, and the color ocean blue.

Secret Gem Remedies

Gemstones and crystals have healing powers based on ancient belief systems. The secrets below come to us from the Chaldeans, who were master astrologers with advanced knowledge of the sun, stars, and our earth, and reveal how to amplify a crystal's power by working with it on a specific day.

Monday: Pearl

Pearls radiate orange rays and operate as a curative if worn on Mondays, starting first thing in the morning. They help with mental wellness, diabetes, colic, and fever.

Tuesday: Ruby

Rubies on Tuesdays are a boon! Ruby heals the heart and carries the red ray of emotional wellness through the expression of love. This is divine energy, and as such there is a striving for the highest love vibration. Ruby brings joy into your life and gives you permission to follow your bliss.

Wednesday: Emerald

Emerald has green light rays and can help with the heart, ulcers, asthma, and influenza, when worn on Wednesday, starting two hours after dawn.

Pearl

Thursday: Topaz

Topaz has blue rays and helps with laryngitis, arthritis, anxiety and upset, fever, and various glandular disorders if worn on Thursdays.

Ruby

Friday: Diamond

Diamonds, containing rays of indigo light, are for eyes, nose, asthma, and laziness, and to prevent drunkenness, especially if worn on Friday. Wearing diamonds in conjunction with a waxing moon enhances their power.

Emerald

Saturday: Sapphire

Sapphire has violet energy. Worn on Saturday on the middle finger of the right hand two hours before sunset, the stone is said to help the kidneys, epilepsy, and sciatica.

Topaz

Sunday: Opal

Sundays are a holy day, when you will come into your soul's true purpose by wearing opal jewelry with its rainbow-colored rays.

Diamond

Sapphire

Opal

Walking the Pagan Path

For centuries, in group rituals and solo spells, witches have walked specific paths in the form of symbolic shapes that hold potent spiritual meaning. All you need for this ritual is a stone that brings you special inspiration.

Maybe it is your birthstone; perhaps it is your jade talisman or calming quartz or intuition-boosting amethyst or labradorite. Put the stone in your pocket and you are ready. You may find one walking pattern to be especially enriching for you. I recommend walking the figure eight, the "eternity" symbol from the magician card in the tarot deck. Otherwise, choose from among the universal shapes below. I suggest always walking sunwise, or clockwise. It can be a distance of your choice, in your living room, a bigger shape in your own backyard or whatever feels right to you, intuitionally. For the more complicated patterns you can draw them on paper and place it where you can see it to use as a guide:

Oval: The shape that designates the spirit and divine being.

Circle: The shape of the sun and moon, designates the whole, the complete, that which never ends and encompasses all.

Cross: The form of a human figure with arms outstretched from the center. The importance of this symbol predated Christianity by millennia.

Hexagram: In the Jewish tradition, the beloved. It is two triangles intersecting, the meeting of heaven and earth.

Five-pointed Star: This resembles the human form with arms and legs outspread—Leonardo Da Vinci's favorite.

Prepare for your pagan pilgrimage, your walking meditation, when the moon is in Sagittarius, Aquarius, or your natal moon sign. These prayer walks represent a journey to our own center and back again out into the world, some of the inner work we witches need to do now and again. Keep your eyes closed for the first step, then open your eyes and pray aloud:

Guide my steps; help me to walk in wisdom.
What I seek on this day, I shall find as I go
With an open heart and mind.
Today, I receive the blessings of the sun.

CEREMONIAL CRYSTAL KNIFE

Athames, as you know, are not for cutting but for raising and managing energy. Athames that have been carved from crystals have become popular in recent years and can be very pretty. Consider these stones to be carved and polished and used as your sacred tool:

Amethyst opens up psychic abilities.

Azurite with malachite incites brilliance.

Celestite brings angel-powered insight and advice.

Selenite is a stone of good fortune in the future.

Amethyst

Change Your Life with Sacred Stones

It is useful to give a lot of thought to the constructive changes that you wish to see in your life, or the positive qualities that you want to develop further in yourself. Crystals and sacred stones can be a great source of clarity, and can help to process emotions. For example, if you want to become more organized, look out for lazulite. Of course, getting organized requires some letting go and getting rid of belongings that have seen better days. This used to be a real problem for me, as any of my friends can tell you, and my cozy cottage is lined with magazines, journals, and books, books, books! But I really felt the need to declutter my life and streamline it—to become a bit more Zen. So, I had to get organized with lazulite power and then let go with lepidolite!

I have never really had any jade but, recently, I've felt the grounding and stabilizing effects of this stone are what I need. I must also become more prosperity- minded. I need to be better about saving money and thinking in terms of my future security, so I'm not reading tarot cards out on the sidewalk when I'm 90! For this reason I've been walking through San Francisco's Chinatown and feeling very attracted to different jades.

I'm sure you feel such urges and attractions, too. This might be your subconscious giving you a gentle nudge about some growing you need to do. Listen to those inner voices, and you will reap the benefits again and again.

Lazulite

THE EFFECTS OF SACRED STONES

Amber for grounding

Aventurine for creative visualization

Bloodstone for abundance and prosperity

Carnelian for opening doors for you and your family

Citrine for motivation and for attracting money
and success

Hematite for strength and courage

Jade, a harbinger of purity and tranquility, to help
you simplify your home and life

Jasper for stability

Lazulite for decluttering, clearing away blocks,
and helping to organize your mind

Lepidolite (which should be called the letting-go stone)
to help you get rid of old habits

Rhodochrosite for staying on course with your
life's true purpose

Watermelon tourmaline for help with planning
your best possible future

Aventurine

Bloodstone

Carnelian

Citrine

Hematite

Lepidolite

Rhodochrosite

Altars

An altar is a physical point of focus for your rituals and should contain a collection of symbolic objects that are assembled in a meaningful manner. Altars can be created for different purposes. A house magic altar in your home provides a space where you honor the rhythms of the season and the rhythms of your own life and household, or you can set up an altar for a specific purpose—for example, nurturing your relationship.

CREATING YOUR HOUSE MAGIC ALTAR

Your house magic altar can be a low table, the top of a chest, or even a shelf. First, smudge the space with the smoke of a sage bundle or by burning sweetgrass or copal. Then cover the altar with your favorite fabric in a color you adore and place a candle in each corner. I like to use candles of many colors to represent the rainbow array of gems.

Place your chosen gems and crystals around the candles. Rose quartz is a heart stone, and fluorite is a calming crystal, so these are good options for grounding yourself, particularly if your altar is in your bedroom, as many are.

Add fresh flowers, incense you love to smell, and any objects that have special meaning for you. Some people place lovely shells or feathers they have found on their paths or while at the beach, and others use imagery that is special— a goddess statue or a star shape, perhaps.

The most important point is that your altar should be pleasing to your eye and your sensibilities. You should feel that it represents the deepest aspects of you as a person.

BLESSING YOUR HOUSE MAGIC ALTAR

Before using your altar for spell work and rituals, it's important to perform a rite of blessing. Bless your altar during a new moon. Light the candles and incense, and say aloud:

Here burns happiness about me.

Peace and harmony are in abundance,

Here my happiness abounds.

Gems and jewels, these bones of the earth,

Bring love, prosperity, health, and mirth.

Be it ever thus that joy is the light

That here burns bright. Blessed be!

You have now consecrated your altar. It connects you to the earth, of which you and all gems and crystals are part, and it will connect you to the house magic that has now entered your life. The more you use it, the more powerful your spells will be.

Lunar Altarations

I often switch up my altar adornments every two or three days with the changing of the lunar cycles. Here are some suggestions for altar combinations and activities in accordance with the moon phases.

New Moon Mini Altar

Add orange candles, yellow jade, neroli essential oil, and cinnamon incense for joy, success, strength, and creativity. Write and speak goals. This is the time to let go of old ways and take up new directions.

Waxing Moon Mini Altar

Add green candles, peridot, clary sage essential oil, and jasmine incense for prosperity, expansion, and healing. Speak your new hopes.

Half-Moon Mini Altar

Add brown candles, tiger eye, and amber oil and incense for grounding and stability. Hold your focus and feel your rootedness to Earth.

Waxing Gibbous Moon Altar

Add red candles, garnet, and rose essential oil and incense for this time to enjoy your life, relax, and let go. Simply be.

Full Moon Mini Altar

Add blue candles, amethyst, bergamot essential oil, and sandalwood incense for this phase of maximum healing and transformation. Seeds planted in the new moon will now come into fruition.

Magical Workings

Your altar is key to your magical workings, so it needs to be infused with YOU. Here is where you can fully apply your personal design and creativity. Tap into your intuition and let it be your guide in this sacred shrine. Select objects that appeal to you symbolically to place on your altar.

Crystals may include rose quartz, amethyst, quartz crystal, or turquoise, or any other minerals that promote healing and add supportive energy during your process. I have a candlestick of purest amethyst crystal, my birthstone. When I gaze on the candle flame refracted through the beautiful purple gemstone, I feel the fire within me.

You should decorate your altar until it is utterly and completely pleasing to your eye. The ritual of creating an altar provides support to your process, and inculcates your altar with the magic that lives inside you, that lives inside all of us, and magnifies the ceremonial strength of your workspace. After you've been working spells for a while, an energy field will radiate from your altar; it will become your true north.

Rose quartz   **Amethyst**   **Quartz crystal**   **Turquoise**

CHAPTER 2

Sacred Space and Magical Protection

Clear a Space
and Make It Yours

To clear and purify your space with as much of your own personal energy as possible, perform a ritual sweeping with a favorite broom or "besom." I use a sweet-smelling cinnamon broom. These are actually made of pine straw, coated with divine-smelling cinnamon oil, and set aside to dry for 3 weeks. Many a grocery store sells them in the fall and holiday season. The smaller ones make lovely gifts, and great altar adornments. I ornament mine with cleansing crystals by stringing a colored silk cord with quartz beads, or gluing the beads to the base of the broom handle.

GEMS FOR SPACE-CLEARING

Amber for positivity and happiness

Onyx as a guardian stone and protector

Tiger's eye to protect from "psychic vampires"
(energy-draining situations or people)

Blue lace agate for serenity and
a peaceful home

Petrified wood for tranquility and a
sense of security

Turquoise to create calm and
facilitate relaxation

Coral for well-being and good cheer

Jet to absorb bad energy from
your environment

Clear quartz for peace of mind
and space-clearing

Amber

Tiger's eye

Blue lace agate

Jet

Petrified wood

Crystal Feng Shui

Stones left in strategic places around your home can help to accelerate the change you desire. Using what I call "crystal feng shui," you can place a crystal or a geode in a particular position in your home to bring about specific results. Below are a few stone placements to try.

GEMS FOR FENG SHUI

Amethyst placed on your nightstand will promote healing and release any negative energy that is clinging to your home.

Jade or yellow "lemon quartz" in clusters on your desk or workspace will activate vibrations of abundance and creativity.

Citrine placed on the left-hand side of your desk will bring more money into your home or office.

Obsidian in a ball can absorb negative energy— try putting it in a dark hallway that seems spooky, or any area where the energy seems very static or low.

Rose quartz can be placed anywhere in your bedroom to make it a place of bliss and unconditional love.

Yellow quartz

Candled Crystals

I made candles as a young girl, and that hobby has now grown into a full-blown obsession. A few years ago, it occurred to me that I could make "stained-glass" candles by mixing big crystal chunks into the wax in the mold. An even easier way to do this is to stud the top and sides of a soft beeswax pillar candle with crystal pieces that cost just pennies per pound from New Age stores. I save them from the melted candles and use them again and again!

STAINED-GLASS SPELL

Recently, I have been wishing and hoping for peace in this world of ours—as have most of us, I am sure. I have been making, burning, and giving away candles with the word "peace" written with crystals embedded in the soft wax.

If possible, perform this spell during a full-moon night for the greatest effect. Place a stained-glass peace candle on your altar and light some rose incense, which represents love and unity. Light the candle and chant:

> I light this candle for hope,
> I light this candle for love,
> I light this candle for unity,
> I light this candle for the good of all the world,
> That we should live in peace. And so it shall be.

Sit in front of your altar, close your eyes, and meditate for a few minutes while visualizing peace in the world. Let the candle burn down completely for the full magical effect.

Rite for Welcoming Spirits

We can all use more benevolent energy in our lives. Some angels may take human form, such as a friend who is always there in a crisis. Others are hovering above in the ether and can be invoked with a few words and a focused intention. Use this spell when you need a guiding hand and angelic assistance.

GATHER TOGETHER

Celestite

1 white and 1 blue candle (these are angelic hues)

rosemary essential oil

frankincense and myrrh incense

celestite, a sky-blue crystal associated with angel energy
(amethyst can substitute)

Anoint both candles with the rosemary essential oil. Light the white candle and use it to light the incense. If you were unable to acquire any frankincense or myrrh incense, you can use rosemary incense or light a rosemary branch in a fireproof glass or clay dish. Now light the blue candle with the white one and place them on either side of the crystal. Breathe deeply and speak this spell aloud to invoke the celestial guardians.

Guardians, I call upon you now

To bring aid and angelic blessings

By earth and sky, I invite you now

To point me to all that is good

And protect me from all that is not.

With gratitude to the heavenly host.

So mote it be.

Angel Protection Charm

In your travels along the sacred path, you doubtless have gathered up many natural treasures, such as seashells, driftwood, crystals, and small pebbles. You can create a simple "Angel Accessing Tool" from your collection of nature's blessings. Here's how to make an amulet any time you want to gather up the good energy of those unseen who can help and protect you (and drive away the not-so-helpful energy).

GATHER TOGETHER

sections of string, at least 6 in (15 cm) in length,
one for each crystal

small chunks of crystal (celestite, amethyst, aquamarine, muscovite,
morganite, and selenite can all help you make contact
with your guardian angels)

a stick (a small piece of sea-smoothed driftwood is perfect)

Tie a piece of string around each chunk of crystal. Attach each string to your stick of wood so the crystals are hanging from the stick. Hang your amulet anywhere in your home you want to "make contact."

Once you have crafted your magical tool, you should store it in a safe place and bring it out when you really need angelic intervention. When I lived in a big city that had lots of car break-ins, I made one for my car and the era of broken windows ended for me. I recommend one for your office space, too. We all need work angels! You can welcome unseen and benevolent spirits into your home and life with this conjuring charm.

Burning Away
Bad Luck Spell

Your kitchen is the heart of your home, your sanctuary. Yet the world is constantly coming in and bringing mundane energy over your threshold—problems at the workplace, financial woes, bad news from your neighborhood or the world at large. All this negativity wants to get in the way and stay. While you can't do anything about the stock market crash in China or a co-worker's divorce, you can do something about not allowing this bad energy to cling to you by using this home-keeping spell.

The best times to release any and all bad luck are on a Friday 13th or on any waxing moon. Get a big black candle and a black crystal, a piece of white paper, a black pen with black ink, and a cancellation stamp, readily available at any stationery store. Go into your backyard or a nearby park or woodlands and find a flat rock that has a slightly concave surface to create a stone altar. Using the pen, write down on the white paper that of which you want to rid yourself and your home; this is your release request. Place the candle and the black crystal on the rock; light the candle, and while it burns, intone the words of the spell.

> Waxing moon, most wise Selene,
>
> From me this burden please dispel
>
> Upon this night so clear and bright
>
> I release _____ to the moon tonight.

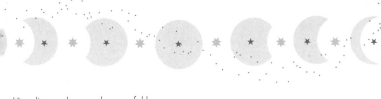

Visualize a clear and peaceful home filled with only positivity as the candle burns for 13 minutes. Stamp the paper with the cancel stamp. Snuff the candle, fold the paper away from your body, and place it under the rock. Speak your thanks to the moon for assisting you. If you have a truly serious issue at hand, repeat the process for 13 nights and all will be vanquished.

ALTAR BOOST

The more use an altar gets, the more energy it builds up, making your spells even more effective and powerful.

Protecting Your Aura

We have all encountered psychic vampires, who tear away little pieces of your chi, or life force, leaving holes in your aura (etheric body). You can identify the places that need patching because they will become noticeably cold as you pass a crystal over them.

Pick your favorite stone from amethyst, citrine, or any quartz and run it all around you at a distance of about 3 in (7.5cm). Make note of the cold spots and lay the crystal on those places for about 5 minutes, until the spot feels warmer. This repairs the holes in your aura and you should begin to feel a pleasant sense of renewed wholeness once again.

Another wonderfully soothing technique is crystal combing. Take a piece of pink kunzite and brush it in gentle, slow, downward strokes from the top of your head, the crown chakra (see page 54), to the bottom of your feet. The next time you feel overwhelmed by anxiety, try this and you will feel more relaxed and in control afterward.

Kunzite is also a heart mender, which works with the heart chakra to bring inner peace, clear away old romantic wounds, and get rid of emotional baggage. While lying down you can place a chunk of kunzite upon your chest, meditate with it, and feel the healing energy flow in.

Pink Kunzite

POWER GEMS FOR EVERYDAY

Amber: One of the oldest of talismans, containing great power for general safety.

Amethyst: Helps with sobriety by preventing inebriation.

Aquamarine: A guard against malevolent spirits, his stone is also useful if you want to attract wisdom or have a fear of water and drowning.

Amethyst

Bloodstone: Lucky and good to wear when traveling.

Carnelian: This stone is to devils what garlic is to a vampire—it keeps 'em away.

Chrysolite: Drives away evil spirits and aids peaceful sleep, especially if set in gold.

Diamond

Diamond: In the form of a necklace, diamonds bring good fortune and should always touch the skin. This dazzling stone works best when it is received as a gift; it lends force and valor.

Emerald: Cancel the power of any magician!

Jade: Offers protection to children and guards their health. Jade also creates prosperity power.

Jasper: Reputed to be a defense against the venom of poisonous insects and snakes.

Jet: Expels negativity, especially when set in silver.

Moonstone: A boon to travelers and also brings fortune and fame.

Protection Magic
with DIY Amulets

Amulets are protective adornments that date back to the beginning of human civilization. They are magical jewelry and the Norse employed them daily, often carving runes on them, directly into the stones and metal. When traveling, they would wear amulets, believing they could guide them if they got lost and keep them safe on the road. Amulets carved with a symbol of the sun, representing the god Thor, were considered very lucky. Evil eye amulets are perhaps the most globally popular, believed in most cultures to be capable of warding off a hex by reflecting it back to its origins. In some cultures, amulets were devoted to a specific god or goddess, and it was thought the wearer would be protected by that divinity. You can make your own amulets for yourself or friends. First, you must select a crystal associated with the energy you wish to manifest—see suggestions opposite.

Hold the crystal in your hand until it gets warm, then visualize the specific power the stone is offering. If the amulet is for you, wear it as a pendant or tuck it in your pocket.

GEMS FOR DIY AMULETS

Aventurine shows new horizons
are ahead

Ruby helps you dare for deep
passion and personal power

Emerald brings prosperity

Sapphire means you will know
the truth

Hematite provides abundance
and groundedness

Snowflake obsidian keeps
troubles at bay

Protective Talismans

A talisman is an object that also provides protection and has magical properties. Ancient peoples, including the Mesopotamians, Assyrians, Babylonians, and Egyptians, loved animal talismans for the qualities associated with different animals for courage—bulls for virility, cats for stealth, and so on.

A talisman can be any article or symbol that you believe has magical properties. As we have discussed, many gems and crystals naturally have very special innate powers. With talismanic magic, the special powers have to be either present through nature or summoned in the context of a ritual in which the magic is instilled. Even though people often confuse amulets with talismans, they differ in this significant way: amulets passively protect the wearer from harm and evil or negativity, while talismans are active in their transformative powers. For example, the supernatural sword Excalibur, a talisman imbued with supremacy by the Lady of the Lake, gave King Arthur magical powers.

Another way to look at it is that talismans are created for a specific task, while amulets have broader uses. So an amulet can be worn all the time for general protection, whereas a talisman is for a specific use and a narrower aim. The varieties of talismans are many: for love, wealth, gambling, the gift of a silver tongue, a good memory, or the prevention of death. Whatever you can think of, there is probably a talisman for that exact purpose!

Amethyst
Circle-of-Protection Ring

A few years ago, a major renaissance in crafting began, starting with knitting, crocheting, and beading. All our grandmothers and great aunts already knew the enormous benefits of such handiwork hobbies but when college students and people of every age started forming knitting circles, it was a remarkable sign. Fun scarves, sweaters, and hats may have been the end product, but crafters widely reported these hobbies to be therapeutic and a real aid to anxiety. Indeed, these handicraft projects and pursuits are very calming. Every moment you wear this sweet bead ring, you will be guided, guarded, and protected. Every gesture you make will be supernatural when you wear your circle-of-protection ring.

Continued overleaf

GATHER TOGETHER

44 tiny amethyst beads, easily available at any craft or bead store

18 in (45 cm) of thin elastic thread (this will accommodate differing finger sizes)

2 sewing or wire-thread needles; make sure they will go through the holes in the beads

multipurpose jewelry glue

Begin by blessing the beads on your altar or workspace:

This gift of the earth so fair,

Stone of serenity, gem so rare,

I call forth all guardians of the air,

Bless these beads and hear my prayer.

Fill each crystal with love and care.

So mote it be.

Next, thread the needles onto each end of the elastic thread and then use one of them to string four beads to the center of the elastic. Thread the left needle through the last bead on the right-hand side. Pull it tight, forming a diamond shape. Next, string one bead on the left thread end and two beads on the right. Thread the left needle through the last bead on the right. Pull it tight. Repeat until all the beads are used. In order to close the ring, thread the left needle through the end bead of the first diamond, instead of the last bead on the right. Pull tight, tie the ring off with a double knot, and place a drop of glue on the knot. Once the glue has dried completely, put on your ring. Notice how everyone is looking as you sparkle by!

CALMING CRYSTAL BEADS

Once you get the knack of this project, you can try it again and vary the number and type of crystal beads. You can also wear more than one for a "stack of serenity."

Lapis lazuli for a keen mind

Moonstone for higher self-esteem

Red coral for a sense of inner strength

Citrine for ease in communicating

Turquoise for tranquility and grounding

Lace agate for feelings of confidence at work

Opal will give you intuition

Rose quartz for love of self and others

A selection of semi precious beads ideal for stringing

Crystal Offering
to the Deities

You can call upon any god or goddess with whom you feel a deep connection, but I advise you take some time to explore. You might be surprised what you discover as there are many deities—some are listed opposite. An unknown god or goddess might help you reveal unseen and unknown sides of yourself. Call on them for rituals, and look for signs and symbols connected to them in your everyday life—they are watching over you.

SPELL TO HONOR THE SUPERNATURAL

Decide what will be a suitable offering to the deity of your choice. If it is a sea spirit, perhaps a beautiful seashell. If it is an earth goddess, a gorgeous crystal would be just right.

Place an offering to your chosen divinity on your altar or shrine—perhaps a verse of poetry or a painting or drawing—that shows your gratitude and appreciation for all you have received and will continue to receive as inspiration. Chant aloud:

O _____ [name of deity], wise and true,

I will walk with thee in the fields of paradise and back.

Anoint me here and now.

Thanks to you, _____ [repeat name of deity], I will never lack.

In gratitude and service, blessed be thee.

GREAT GODS AND GODDESSES

There are many deities you can call upon; here are just a few that can particularly help support your wellbeing.

Ceres

Ceres is the great Roman grain goddess. Think of her every time you have some cereal, which is named after her. The early summer festival, the Cerealia, honors Ceres for supplying the harvest and an abundance of crops. Any ceremony for planting, growing, and cooking could involve this bounty-bringer. If you are going to plant a magical garden, craft a ritual with Ceres and make an outdoor altar to this grain goddess.

Adonis

Adonis does not get nearly enough credit as a god of healing. He is better known as the legendary god of love, and partner of the goddess of love, Aphrodite. Adonis is also an herbal deity with domain over certain plants and flowers, representing earth, fertility, and health. He is often invoked for love rites and spells. Ask Adonis for help with your gardens and for healing.

Osiris

Osiris is the Egyptian god of death and rebirth who also takes care of the crops, the mind, the afterlife, and manners. Husband to Isis and father of Horus, Osiris is a green god who is deeply connected to the cycles of growing and changing seasons. Turn to this god for rites of remembrance and for help with grief and mourning.

Sunna

Sunna is the ancient Germanic goddess of the sun, making clear that the big star in the nearby sky has not always been deified as male. The Teutons also referred to this very important divine entity as the "Glory of Elves." In the great poetic epic, the Eddas, it was said she bore a new daughter Suhn, who sheds light on a brand-new world. Other sun goddesses include the Arabic Atthar, the Celtic Sulis, and the Japanese Amaterasu. As you rise each morning, speak your greeting to Sunna. Morning rituals set a positive tone for the day, ensuring that you are indeed living a magical life.

Aganippe

Aganippe's abode was on Mount Helicon in ancient Greece, in a wellspring that was sacred to the muses. Living in these sacred waters gave Aganippe the ability to confer inspiration upon poets; inspiration flowed as well in the water drunk from the rivers and brooks that had their source in her spring. She is the daughter of the river deity Ternessus. An especially charming part of this myth is that the wellspring was created by the hooves of Pegasus.

The Eye Goddess

The Eye Goddess is an extremely ancient Mediterranean deity. She was a goddess of justice in the form of a pair of huge, unblinking eyes, and no transgression could be concealed from her. The Eye Goddess's first appearance was around 3,500 BCE. You can conjure the Eye Goddess's powers of justice with the depiction of eyes and invoke her assistance any time you need the truth brought to light. You can also practice simple protection magic for the home and for your car with eyes watching out for you. Her symbol is sometimes mistaken for the evil eye, which makes workers of mischief nervous and causes thieves to think twice before committing a crime.

Juno

Juno watches over the daughters of the earth, and as such attends nearly every female need and function. The Latin word for a female soul is juno, and as the mother of all women she can be invoked in any woman's mystery of birth, menses, croning, and death. Some of her aspects include a goddess of fate, Juno Fortuna; of war, Juno Martialis; of marriage, Juno Domiduca; of bones, Juno Ossipaga; of mother's milk, Juno Rumina. Because Juno is a special protector of brides, you can invent a Juno-centered ceremony to celebrate your own nuptials or those of a friend who espouses women's spirituality.

CHAPTER 3

Witchy Wellness
and Calm

Goddess Blessing Ritual

Wherever you are along the pagan path, I have no doubt that you are being called upon to help your loved ones, your spiritual circle, and your community much more than ever before. The pressures of work, finances, constant connectedness, and the unrelenting barrage of negative news reduce immunity. Self-care is essential and, like many of you, I am drawing from everything I have learned from my magical mentors and all my experience and Book of Shadows (see page 143) recordings for what works well to counteract the dis-ease in our environment. In times like these, we are called upon to serve others. That is the intention behind this spell.

Amethyst   **Citrine**   **Jade**

GATHER TOGETHER

1 green, 1 brown, and 1 blue candle

1 amethyst, 1 citrine, and 1 green jade crystal

sandalwood incense in a small fireproof bowl

a smooth flat stone, at least 10 in (25 cm) in length

Tapping into the strength of earth is an important aspect of healing magic. This rite is best performed outdoors in the garden or on your fire escape or deck. Take the flat stone and designate it as your outdoor altar. Now, place the candles, crystals, and incense on the rock. Light the first candle, whichever color you prefer, and the incense and pray aloud:

The world is too much with us

But we have the power of our Mother Goddess.

The magic we bring to the world

Will help, will uplift, will serve, will heal.

Mother Goddess, I call upon you to make me a vessel

To help others in times of need. For this, I thank you.

So mote it be. Blessed be.

Light the next candle and repeat the spell. Light the last candle and say it again. Contemplate the candle flames as you draw strength from Mother Earth. You will know when it is time to put out the candles and incense. Store your mobile altar and, when you need to recharge, repeat the wish spell.

Chakra Rainbow Renewal

The Rainbow is a simple and effective method for total-body wellness. For this healing practice, you will need seven stones, one for each color of the rainbow—violet, indigo, blue, green, yellow, orange, and red. Provided opposite is a list of crystals I would suggest using, including their body affinities in case there is a specific area you want to focus on.

The first step for anyone undertaking crystal healing is to lie down, relax, and get very comfortable. Empty your mind of all thoughts, and breathe deeply. Now place your chosen stones on their corresponding chakra centers. I recommend keeping the stones in place for a half hour, but I have seen positive effects take place in just minutes. While you are relaxing, visualize yourself enjoying total wellness, free of the malady you are treating.

1 CROWN CHAKRA

Jadeite for the knees

Dendrite agate for the nervous system

Moonstone for the womb

Purple fluorite for the bone marrow

Amethyst for sobriety

2 THIRD-EYE CHAKRA

Lapis lazuli for the throat

Celestite for the intestines

Calcite for the skeletal system

Fluorite for coordination and balance

3 THROAT CHAKRA

Blue tourmaline for the thymus

Benitoite for the pituitary

Lapis lazuli for the throat

Dioptase for the lungs

Celestite for the intestines

4 HEART CHAKRA

Chrysocolla for the pancreas

Chrysolite for the appendix

Chrysoprase for the prostate

Beryl for the eyes

Moldavite for the hands

Moss agate for circulation and to boost the immune system

5 SOLAR PLEXUS CHAKRA

Calcite for the skeletal system

Jasper for the shins and for the skin

Danburite for the muscles

Fluorite for the teeth

Citrine to protect the aura

6 SACRAL CHAKRA

Amber for the thyroid

Fire agate for the stomach

Coral to calm and soothe nerves

Orange calcite for the bladder

Chalcedony for the spleen

7 ROOT CHAKRA

Bloodstone for the kidneys

Carnelian for the liver

Garnet for the spine

Hematite for the blood and circulatory system

Rose quartz for the heart

Fire agate for the stomach

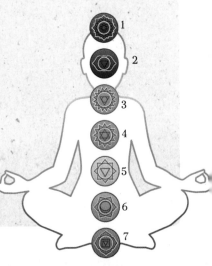

Chakra Healing Crystals

The chakras (see pages 54–55) are energy hotspots on the body. Crystals can help channel positive energy into them and encourage the release of negative energy through them.

Cuprite

This mineral crystal is formed from copper ore and can have needle-like crystals of a brilliant red inside a nearly black crystal. It has a spectacular sparkle. In the same way that copper has wonderful health benefits, so does cuprite, helping with concerns in the heart, blood, skin, muscles, and bones. Cuprite stimulates the lower chakra. It is a handy stone to take on air flights, as it can treat altitude sickness. It also furthers the functions of the bladder and kidneys.

Dioptase

This gorgeous gemstone is nearly the color of emerald but lacks the hardness, thus lowering its marketplace value. The true value of dioptase lies in its ability to help anyone experiencing mental stress. It lends balance to male and female energies and acts as a stabilizer. As an energy stone, dioptase can activate and awaken all of the chakras. When you wear dioptase, you will fascinate admirers with this beautiful stone and find peace of mind in the process.

Selenite

This chakra healer helps rid unhealthy and negative thoughts, yours or others', from your mind and etheric body. It is a record-keeping stone and carries information from the centuries on Earth it has witnessed. It can also be placed over the third eye to access stored information about your past lives. In the same way this crystal retains, it is good for letting go and helps you forgive. Selenite can also be used for healing of the nerves, reproductive organs, and spine, lending flexibility. With its white swirls, selenite can give an enormous boost to creative visualization, and can be a most auspicious crystal ball for gazing.

Sugilite

Another forgiveness and letting-go stone, sugilite is so powerful that it can help with channeling. Placed on the third-eye area, it alleviates sadness and despondency, and protects your very soul from the frustration and disillusionment of this world. This healing stone dispels headaches and gently draws pain out of afflicted areas, bringing respite to inflammations, toxicity, and stress-related illness. Sugilite has been used to great effect to ease the discomfort of those suffering from cancer. This stone also absorbs anger, hurt, and energies that you have unwittingly picked up and are draining you. If you have problems with jealousy, it helps you rise above any pettiness and bring out your best side. I love that sugilite creates a sense of belonging for those who always felt like outsiders.

Turquoise

This opens the heart chakra and also affords a heart-centered quality, a loving connection with others. Turquoise releases negative emotions and draws out unsettling vibrations. After using turquoise as a "drawing stone," place it on the ground afterward, because the earth can absorb and process the negativity that is no longer inside you. Turquoise will help you find your deepest, truest self: it inspires and uplifts, offering elevation to the chakras. The properties of this stone are as practical as they are spiritual—igniting intuition and enabling the wearer to grow toward wholeness. As a healer, turquoise can be placed gently upon an area of affliction for quick pain relief. It is especially helpful for headaches.

Rocks that Restore the Body

The simplest way to access healing with crystal is to wear a stone. While you are enjoying the considerable benefits to your wellbeing conferred by crystals, you can also appreciate the unmatched beauty provided by Mother Nature herself.

Brightening albite

Albite is the sister of the polished moonstone. A milky-colored stone with blue shading, it can be found in Africa, Europe, and the Americas. Albite is helpful for the immune system and breathing problems, and can assist the spleen and thyroid. This translucent stone calms the wearer and fights depression. A chunk of albite in your bedroom will help banish the blues.

Amazing amethyst

Amethyst is one of the stones most esteemed by healers. The legendary American psychic Edgar Cayce recommended it for control and temperance. Amethyst is believed to aid in the production of hormones and regulate the circulatory, immune, and metabolic systems. It is treasured for its centering and calming properties and seems to connect directly to the mind, fighting emotional swings and depression. Aquarians and Pisceans can count it as their birthstone. Amethyst also helps with mental focus, intuition, meditation, and memory.

Awesome aventurine

Aventurine is one of those rare general healers that can offer wellness to any part of the body upon which it is laid. As a general healing stone, it can also be used in tandem with other stones, such as rose quartz and malachite. Combined with rose quartz, aventurine can help open your heart and soul to love and compassion. Used in combination with malachite, the benefits are clarity and raised consciousness. Highly recommended and an excellent boon for young children, aventurine is a wonder stone for the wellbeing of the whole family.

Boosting bloodstone

Bloodstone is a recent name for this powerful restorative. The ancient name for this variegated chalcedony quartz is "heliotrope." It stands to reason that bloodstone would be connected with blood and the circulatory system. It is also used to detoxify the liver, kidneys, and spleen. In India, bloodstone is ground up and taken in an elixir as an aphrodisiac. A belief stemming from ancient times is that bloodstone can give great courage and help avoid harmful situations. All in all, bloodstone enriches the blood, calms the mind, and increases the consciousness of the wearer. This is a great gem for you if you have a sedentary and detail-oriented job.

Calming calcite

Calcite is helpful to bones and joints and is a memory booster. In addition to aiding the retention of information, calcite is a calming agent that can bring clarity to decision-making processes. Green calcite is a terrific support to people in transition, bringing about positive energy in place of the negative. The yellow and gold calcites are useful for meditation thanks to their association with the sun, light, the sign of the spiritual path, and higher knowledge. It is said that these sunny calcites can even help with astral projection. Calcite is a healing stone and is highly recommended for physicians, nurses, and healers to keep at their offices.

Green calcite

Yellow calcite

Chakra-enhancing carnelian

Carnelian is linked with the lower chakras, can heal holes in the etheric body, and can give support for letting go of anger, old resentments, and emotions that no longer serve a positive purpose. Orange carnelian is especially beloved for its ability to promote energy and vitality by warming the emotions. If worn at your throat, carnelian overcomes timidity and lends the power of great and eloquent speech. Like some other red stones, it also gives you courage. In addition, wearing carnelian can offer you a sense of comfort and create the proper atmosphere for meditation and total clarity of mind and thought. Carnelian as a pendant or on a belt gives you control of your thoughts and understanding of others.

Curative chrysocolla

Chrysocolla is a stone associated with Gaia, our Earth Mother, and also Kwan Yin, the benevolent bringer of compassion. Chrysocolla evokes the qualities of these goddesses: nurture, forgiveness, and tolerance. It is viewed as a lunar stone, perfect for meditations with the new moon and on global issues such as the environment and world peace. By merely holding this placid piece of earth in your hand, you can send healing energy out to the planet.

Medicinal moss agate

Moss agate is usually a dark color: brown, black, or blue. Moss agate comes from India, North America, or Australia. It is named as such because it has patterning in light-colored clusters that resembles moss. This is a cleansing stone and can bring balance to both sides of the brain, therefore reducing depression or emotional ailments. Moss agate is also useful for treating hypoglycemia. It is the stone of farmers, botanists, and midwives—those who nurture new life. It also aids intuition and creativity and can reduce inhibition and shyness, so it is great to wear if you are a speaker, singer, or performer.

Releasing rhodonite

Rhodonite aligns the physical, emotional, and mental facets of your entire being and brings balance to them. If you are feeling ungrounded and scattered, this crystal will soothe and uplift. This confidence crystal can help you attain your greatest potential. The highest-grade gem form of rhodonite awakens the intuition. As a healer, rhodonite alleviates the shock that accompanies a grievous loss. It is also used for issues involving the ears and hearing and is said to be very good for bone growth. Rhodonite helps build a healthy emotional foundation, and I think the best and highest use of rhodonite is for healing old emotional wounds and scars, letting you grow from the experience. If you are feeling low-grade anxiety, this is an excellent crystal to carry in your pocket as a touchstone.

HEALING CRYSTAL RINGS

Malachite on your right hand to prevent burnout and restore you.

Opal on your right hand and your wellness wishes will be granted!

Onyx on your left hand for relieving stress and quieting the mind.

Moonstone with a silver setting boosts your self-regard and optimism.

Red garnet overcomes lethargy and engenders a new lease on life.

Jasper helps heal the skin and maintain a youthful appearance.

Citrine helps with stomach aches and mental clarity, and increases powers of concentration.

Pearls are very soothing and will calm headaches and uplift you.

Mineral Medicine

Since the dawn of humankind, people have carried stones and crystals as helpers and as talismans; for protection and good luck. In so doing, they have brought themselves a greater sense of security. For peace of mind, the strongest "medicine" consists of a turquoise, a rhodochrosite, and an amethyst. While they may sound exotic, they are commonly available in metaphysical stores.

GATHER TOGETHER

a small sky-blue bag

a turquoise crystal

a rhodochrosite crystal

an amethyst crystal

Place the crystals in the bag. When you are ready, hold the pouch in your hand and incant:

Stones of the earth, warmed by the sun,

Clear away trouble, Help and healing is now begun.

I recommend leaving your pouch on your altar where it can be at the ready whenever needed.

Turquoise

Rhodochrosite

Amethyst

Awesome Altar Stones

Crystals are finally being acknowledged for their power to give greater physical strength and health, and can be added to your healing altar. Turquoise stones are grounding, and agates raise the energy level. For good circulation, try carnelian. For keeping life on an even keel, the organic gem family—shells, corals, and abalone—is optimal. For impetus and motivation, work with carnelian. To boost your health and well-being, try red coral for the lungs, bloodstone for the heart, and moonstone during pregnancy.

INSTANT INSPIRATION

To lift your spirits, light a green candle and hold harmony-bringing jade while meditating.

•

Carrying a quartz crystal will create tranquility inside and around you.

•

If you're feeling overwhelmed or under duress, hold black obsidian. If the stress is caused by an overabundant workload, keep the obsidian on your desk. Obsidian absorbs the negative.

Crystalline Calm

You can create a sense of blissful and composed calm with the following spell.

Timing: The spell works best during early morning or twilight, when the light is half sun and half dark.

Sit with a turquoise stone for grounding in your left hand and with clear quartz in your right hand for calm and clarity. Feel the cool stones begin to warm to your hand and meditate in the quietude of half-light. Then speak this spell:

Fear and doubt leave me now.

Serenity and strength, come to me now.

In these stones, I feel the earth, the mountain.

I receive my vitality from Nature, grounding now.

Now and in the future, all joy will enter.

Harm to none, only good. Blessed be me.

Keep the two stones on your nightstand for whenever you need to regain calm and clarity.

A Grounding Ritual

Simplicity is the key to the effectiveness of this rite. All you need is
a candle and a rock.

GATHER TOGETHER

1 brown candle

1 moss agate or other earth stone (see page 66 for suggestions)

Take the candle and crystal and place them both on the floor. Light the candle
and sit in front of it with your stone in your hand. Touch your stone to your
forehead and say aloud:

> Worry and fear
>
> Are no longer here.
>
> This is my touchstone, strong and true,
>
> Come what may, I have the power to renew.
>
> With harm to none and blessings to all,
>
> So mote it be.

Now close your eyes and hold the stone in both your hands. Notice how
a feeling of grounding rises up through your body to the top of your head.
I keep my moss agate on my work shrine and if times are especially intense
or worrisome, I carry it with me, just as it is or in a little bag.

EARTH STONES FOR CENTERING

Moss agate: This is quartz that has a plantlike pattern caused by metallic crystalline grains. It is a power stone associated with the metal-rich planet Mercury and all things related to the mind. It makes a great grounding stone for anyone who can get too caught up in their thoughts, and is a wonderful crystal for those who need help in keeping their feet on the ground.

Jasper: This stone has been valued for its healing and grounding energies since ancient times. Jasper stones carry very strong earth energy, helping to deepen your personal connection with the earth when you wear or meditate with them. I recommend either brown or red jasper, both of which are healing stones that also give you great strength, heighten energy, and have a lovely reinvigorating effect on your body.

Smoky quartz: Smoky quartz is another beautifully grounding and stabilizing crystal that brings powerful energies for centering the body. This particular quartz has the effect of making you feel deeply rooted to the earth. It is very centering in an uplifting way, having a much subtler energy than hematite. Smoky quartz works to counteract any negative vibrations, replacing them with the positive.

K2: This crystal has recently become more popular, but it will be a new discovery and a revelation for many people. K2 is a combination of grounding granite and celestial azurite, which balances our earthbound life experiences with our higher consciousness and connection to the universe and the heavens. It is an extremely powerful way to connect to your intuition and find the balance between your intuition and your daily life. If you are wrestling with a real issue in your life or need to make a difficult choice where the options are unclear to you, call upon K2 and use it in meditation. Soon, the answers will come.

Shungite: Here is the most powerful stone for balancing. Shungite will inspire you to deal with your emotions, toxic thoughts, and anything that no longer serves you. While it can be unpleasant to look at these personal issues, it is a healthy thing to do. What you gain from this exercise is the grace and strength to cut the energetic cords that hold you back from your personal power.

Moss agate

Jasper

Smoky quartz

K2

Shungite

Let Go with Lepidolite

Lepidolite should be called the letting-go stone. It's like a fresh breeze coming into a room filled with stale air. This uncommon mica, an ore of lithium, has only recently come onto the gem and mineral market. It is shiny and plate-like in appearance, usually occurring in a pretty, pearly pink or purple color. On occasion, it appears white, and very rarely, it shows up in gray or yellow. This mineral occurs in Brazil, Russia, California, and a few spots throughout Africa. My favorite specimens are the single, large sheets of the lovely mica, which are called books and are an unforgettable violet.

Lepidolite is a great stone for getting a handle on anger issues. It soothes unresolved resentments, hatred, and frustrations. It is another mental stone and amplifies thoughts. Lepidolite is almost like a fairy stone in that it attracts positive energy, brightens spirits, and increases intuition. This is one powerful chakra healer, particularly for the heart and base chakras. One of the most important uses for this stone, albeit with great care, is for healing issues resulting from incest. Lepidolite is so powerful that you can even help manic depression and schizophrenia with it. When I had a bout of upsetting dreams and nightmares—unusual, as I usually have pleasant Piscean dreams—lepidolite came to my aid.

If you are lucky enough to come across a lepidolite that has fused with a rubellite tourmaline, then you have a rare rock indeed, and one that has double the power of any other lepidolite. This mauve mica is a commanding tuner for the etheric body, raising the frequency, tone, and pitch of energy in your head. Chakra healers have reported that lepidolite sends energy in a gentle and profoundly medicinal way from the heart chakra to the crown chakra and back again, strengthening the "cord" attaching the etheric body to our body and soul, and to the here and now.

Emotional Detox Rite

One quick way to deal with negative and hard emotions is with lepidolite's ability to balance emotions and create inner peace.

GATHER TOGETHER
6 small lepidolite stones

1 pink candle

Place six small lepidolite stones in a circle and light a pink candle in the center of the circle. Hold one of the lepidolite stones in your left hand, for heart connection, and concentrate on what is holding you back, both spiritually and psychologically. With each issue, feeling, or concern, say aloud:

I let go of ___

Do this a total of six times for each issue, holding a different crystal each time and placing the stone back in the circle after speaking. Picture the problem going into the stone in your left hand. When you are feeling full of calm energy, usually after about 10 minutes, extinguish the candle and place the stones outside your house (where no one will pick them up) and know that you have rid your home, personal space, and psyche of these woes! Whenever you feel the need, let go with lepidolite!

Lepidolite

Relax with Amethyst

In J. R. R. Tolkien's magical Middle Earth, the Elves wore crystal rings, including the prettiest of purple amethysts. Elves are known for their calm self-possession as well as their brilliant minds and connection to the earth, and to forests in particular. Whenever you're feeling tense or just need a little pick-me-up after a long day, amethyst is a great stone to have at hand. It is known for being the perfect crystal to promote restfulness, bring peace of mind, and calm anxiety. Its purple hue is soothing to the eye and mind, and the energy of the crystal will loosen tension in your body and help you leave the hustle and bustle of the day behind. If you have a favorite tree in your backyard or neighborhood, use this as your serenity station—there you can regain the feeling of being centered enjoyed by the tree-loving Elves.

This is an incredibly simple ritual. All you need do is visit your familiar tree and place your amethyst over the center of your forehead—your Third Eye chakra—to get in touch with the crystal's peaceful energy. Surrender all your cares and let your body be filled with the quiet vibrations of the amethyst.

Rest with Blue Lace Agate

We all slept in our mother's arms and under the loving care of a maternal presence in our early years. A mother's love can still be invoked for a good night's sleep. You can invoke the Norse goddess Nerthus, whose power crystal is blue lace agate. When you feel weary or mentally drained, try this sweet ritual, which is perfect for the everyday insomniac. We have all been there—long nights spent scrolling through social media or web articles, as we wait for exhaustion to creep in and take us, finally, to the realm of dreams. Even when we know that the blue light effect from our screens is self-defeating, keeping us awake even longer! Much better than a late-night "doom-scroll" is picking up a book, meditating, or, better yet, trying this little ritual to prepare your mind for slumber.

Place a blue lace agate between your palms before going to sleep. It will empty your mind and fill your bedroom with a restful energy to lull you to sleep. Breathe slowly and deeply, letting your eyes flutter shut. When you feel a calm beginning to settle over you, whisper to yourself: "Nerthus, goddess of night and mother to us all, give me deep sleep. On this night I shall slip into blissful slumber. In gratitude to you, blessed be." Then place the stone under your pillow or beside your bed and prepare yourself for a long, deep sleep.

Calming Cure
to Heal from Hurt

To help heal yourself from a major upset in life, try this soothing potion that uses rose quartz powerful healing qualities for physical and emotional health.

GATHER TOGETHER

¼ cup (60 ml) jojoba or almond base oil

small dark-colored sealable bottle

4 drops rose essential oil

4 drops vanilla essential oil

4 drops clove essential oil

4 tiny rose quartz crystals

handkerchief or cotton ball

Pour the base oil into the bottle and add the essential oils. Seal the bottle and then gently shake it to mix. Now add the rose quartz crystals into the vial. Pour a few drops of the mixture onto the handkerchief or cotton ball and dab it lightly on your temples, neck, and shoulders, gently rubbing in a circular motion. Silently call upon Venus to assist you. Keep the calming oil to use any time you need tranquility; it should last at least six months if kept in a cool, dry cupboard.

Elixir of Enchantment

Adding a tiny crystal to potions harnesses the energy of the crystal. Amethyst is a calming crystal that will add serenity to your space in a home mister.

GATHER TOGETHER

1-fluid ounce (30-ml) blue spray bottle

distilled water

small amethyst crystal

3 drops vanilla essential oil

3 drops neroli essential oil

Fill the bottle three quarters full with the distilled water. Drop in the tiny crystal so it floats down to the bottom of the bottle. Add the neroli and vanilla essential oils and seal the bottle. Shake it gently. Before spraying around your home, chant aloud:

This is a home of peace.

This is a home of happiness.

Happiness lives here.

Healthiness lives here.

And so it is.

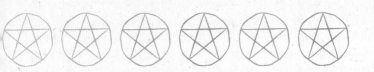

CHAPTER 4

Personal Power and Inspiration

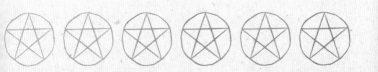

The Power of Sacred Stones

During my childhood, I loved walking around woods looking for flowers, rocks, and all manner of trees. Pretty crystals with unusual shapes or colorations would catch my eye, and I would come back home from my Thoreau-esque wanderings with my pockets filled. At the age of 11, I read J. R. R. Tolkien's *The Hobbit* and then immediately dived into *The Lord of the Rings*. Now, Tolkien understood the power of crystals and gems, and he contributed greatly to their legend and lore. I remember reading enviously about the Dwarves' glittering caves and treasure troves. For me, it was no mystery that the One Ring was evil, because it was a plain band inscribed with the language of Mordor in Elvish script and with no stones at all, while the rings of the heroic Elrond, Gandalf, Galadriel, and Aragorn all featured beautiful stones.

So, stones and gems were good and had the power to help vanquish evil? Yep, this I could completely understand. Even in the lavish and incredibly entertaining movie versions of this epic book series, stones have a starring role; I think I especially enjoyed when Gandalf claps a big quartz crystal onto his wizard's staff to light the way. I was also delighted to discover that Tolkien's Middle Earth was akin to Europe and England, covering much of the north. Indeed, the great scribe's fantasy was largely informed by his study of the folklore of what is now Scandinavia, whose people prized metals, fossils, petrified tree crystals, and all manner of magical rocks. The Norse were a practical people with a passion for the sacred. They had to be pragmatic to survive the cold, harsh northern climate for many months, but every aspect of their life was enhanced by Mother Nature's gift of gems and crystals. This mythos and magical intent were woven into their traditions. For example, amber, the crystal formed from a tree's golden resin, is known as "Freya's Tears" and regarded as holy and healing to widows, while diamonds are sparks of Thor's lightning. This reverence for gems and crystals appears throughout Norse magic.

Onyx for Optimism

Onyx possesses a lot of earth energy, as shown by its usually very dark, often black, color. It has been used for centuries, even in building and for weapons (in the form of arrowheads in the northern kingdoms). Onyx holds memories and secrets, retaining a physical record of what happens around it; therefore, it can be regarded as a story stone. It is super stable and shares this strength with people who need it. It is particularly good for athletes and those who do physical labor. Healers recommend that onyx be worn only on the left side of the body, or on a chain so it hangs at the center of the body over the heart or solar plexus areas. Onyx is best for relieving stress and quietening the mind. This is a generous rock in that it creates goodwill and self-confidence.

I give talks at metaphysical bookstores and conferences, which can make me worry whether I will do a good job, explain myself well, and do justice to the topic. I have an onyx bracelet that I wear for these occasions which gives me the confidence I need. If you have a forthcoming event that is making you nervous, or a very thorny or difficult task at hand, adorn yourself with an onyx ring, bracelet, or pendant—things will run more smoothly and you'll feel more optimistic about what you're facing as a result.

Refresh with Red Jasper

A Norse legend has it that the great dragon-slayer Siegfried was able to handle the mighty winged beast because of the red jasper in his shield. And yes! This pretty scarlet stone can help you greet each day with greater personal power. This ritual is best performed at the beginning of the week, or any time you need an extra burst of motivation. Red jasper is an excellent stone for relieving stress and to help you ground yourself. Let this stone unleash your inner warrior, giving you the endurance that you need to get through the day, week, or difficult task that has been getting you down.

Take the red jasper stone in your hand and focus on its energies. For one minute, contemplate areas of your life where you feel you need a little extra motivation to pull through. Perhaps it's just another Monday, or you're feeling bogged down with work, or a creative block is preventing you from moving forward with your goals. While you have that situation in mind, allow a feeling of encouragement from the jasper to fill you. Know that you are not alone and that a warrior lives within you, ready to take charge in your life.

Boost with Blue Apatite

This sky-blue stone can send blue moods and negativity away and help you maintain a healthy, day-to-day attitude. Blue apatite rules over willpower, affecting your resolve and inspiring you to create and sustain positive change in your life. If you have ever struggled to keep your New Year's exercise, self-care, or healthy-eating resolutions, this ritual is exactly what you need. Start with just one goal that you wish to focus on to improve your health. Maybe that goal is going for a walk every other day or drinking your eight daily cups of water.

Whatever your goal, let that be your intention as you hold the crystal in your palm. Focus on the motivational power of the blue apatite and allow it to create a determined spirit within you and help you believe in your ability to achieve your health goals. From this moment on, keep the crystal close to you, and let it serve as a reminder of your goal and your promise to yourself.

Hematite to Vanquish Anxiety

Hematite shores up self-image and self-belief. It also transforms negative energy into positive. Hematite is considered to be yang, a more male energy. My preferred aspect of this shiny wonder is that it assists with both legal problems and astral projection. Hematite is a creativity crystal and a marvelous mental enhancer, increasing the ability to think with logic, to focus, to concentrate, and to remember more clearly and completely. Hematite draws anxiety out of the body and creates calm.

In addition to all of these outward-projecting aspects, hematite contributes to inner work: self-knowledge, deeper consciousness, and wisdom. Like the iron in the earth from which it is formed, hematite grounds. If you feel spacey or disconnected, you should wear hematite. Hematite contains tremendous grounding energy that makes you feel like you are literally one with the earth. Touch it to your skin and feel the magnetic energy. It is this effect that will make you feel more balanced, calm, and centered. Hematite stones also soak up any negative energy within your body or energy field. After you have used it, you should place the stone in a bowl of pure salt to cleanse it.

Flourish with Fluorite

Any fluorite reduces electromagnetic pollutants and cleanses the aura. Get a big chunk of fluorite at your favorite metaphysical five-and-dime/pound store and put it right beside your computer to decrease stress. Those long hours of staring at the screen will cease to sap your energy. Look at your fluorite at least once an hour to reduce eye and brain strain, too!

YOUR CHOICE OF CLEANSING

Violet—or amethyst—colored fluorite is especially good for the bones, including the marrow. This crystal opens the third eye and, best of all, imparts good old common sense!

Green fluorite is favored for its ability to ground and center excessive physical and mental energy.

Clear fluorite awakens the crown chakra and helps you to let go of anything preventing spiritual development.

Blue fluorite facilitates mental clarity, orderly thought, and the ability to be a master communicator.

Yellow fluorite kindles the synapses and awakens memory. It will also make you smarter and boosts your creativity.

Powerful Calcite

The ancients believed that calcite placed at the base of a pyramid could amplify its power. The Bosporus, one of the first sites where calcite was mined and gathered, was also raided early on by Gothic tribes and then later by the Huns, led by the legendary chief Attila. After discovering the healing power of calcite, the Celts collected this stone, which was often to be found in caves. It strengthens the bones and functions as an aid to psychics. For the magical folk of today, calcite provides a powerful boost to psychism—for example, it can be worn during tarot readings for greater intuition.

Remarkably, calcite can be used to increase intelligence and clarify the emotions at the same time. If a relationship or work situation is confusing, and you don't understand another person's intentions or behavior, meditation with calcite will clear that difficulty up and give you complete transparency.

The Efficiency of Beryl

Beryl has a most unusual and important healing asset—it prevents people from doing the unnecessary. Furthermore, it helps the wearers to focus and to remove distractions, and therefore become calmer and more positive. Beryl also strengthens the liver, kidneys, and intestines, as well as the pulmonary and circulatory systems. It is especially effective for the throat and is invaluable for those who have to talk a lot in their work. Some crystal healers use beryl along with lapis lazuli as a sedative for nervous conditions. If you get overwhelmed at work or have a huge task ahead of you, efficiency-enhancing beryl will get you through it.

Listen to Lapis Lazuli

The wise old healers relied on this beautiful blue crystal so much that they ground it up to use in tiny quantities in potions. Lapis lazuli is very nearly second to none as a thought amplifier. It also enhances psychic power and can open the Third Eye chakra when laid very briefly on the forehead over the Third Eye.

Nowadays, almost all of us are overextended and become so busy that we move away from our core. There is a danger in this, as we can move off-track and stop living our lives—instead, our lives end up living us. We can get so caught up in the business of work and home and family obligations that we are not living out our destinies. Lapis lazuli stone will help you stay in touch with your essence, with who you are supposed to become.

Lapis lazuli is a guide to be listened to in absolute stillness. In today's world of endless distraction, this blue gem will help you regain your balance—blue is always the color of peace, spirituality, and tranquility. It is such a powerful healer of the mind and spirit. Wear it for mindfulness and to achieve a sense of wellbeing.

Meditation for Mind and Body

Dive deep into lapis lazuli's blue pool of positive energy when you feel the need to sharpen your mind or if you are feeling worn down and overburdened.

GATHER TOGETHER

blue candle

lapis lazuli crystal

matches

Light the candle and hold the crystal in front of your eyes so you can see the light of the flame gleaming slightly through the stone. Pray aloud:

A quickening runs through me,

I feel the beat of my heart this day.

My soul, body, and mind are as one.

I am whole and hale today and all tomorrows.

And so it is. Blessed be me.

Repeat the spell three times, then extinguish the candle and place the lapis lazuli crystal on your altar. Keep it there for a while for those times you need a pick-me-up.

The Magic of Diamonds

I love the charming legend that Europeans first discovered diamonds from Africa in the pouch of a shaman, who used them for healing magic. Prehistoric peoples believed diamonds were fragments of the stars and the teardrops of the gods. In very ancient times, they were worn as adornment in their rough and unpolished state. As you might imagine, they are thought to bring good luck, but there is another school of thought, held by diamond-phobes, that these gems bring misfortune. The legend of the Hope Diamond from India is a fascinating example of this, as every owner of the royal rock was bankrupted until it was finally nestled in the safe of the Smithsonian Institution in Washington, D.C.

Diamonds are associated with lightning and ensuring victory for the warriors who wore them. They are thought to be powerful enough to repel madness and even to stave off the devil himself! The medieval mystic Rabbi Benoni believed that diamonds were conducive to true spiritual joy and had power over the stars and planets in the heavens.

Sacred Speaking Stones

Our voices are one of the most important tools in magic for change. Perhaps you're speaking at a large gathering, where you'll need to project your voice with strength and conviction, or perhaps you're knocking door-to-door, to speak with individuals on a topic you are passionate about. Even at home alone, when chanting the words of a spell, your voice carries power and intention.

An easy way to amplify the power of your voice is with crystals—amber, amethyst, aquamarine, azurite, blue obsidian, blue topaz, blue tourmaline, kunzite, and purple jade are what I call "speaking stones." If you are chanting or speaking in public, wear these stones in chokers or necklaces to manifest a noticeable change for the better.

THE POWER OF PINK

A ring with a pink stone packs a real punch in engendering change. Any finger will work well, but the right gem on your little finger can help you find and pursue new opportunities and change the direction of your whole life. There can be a lot of power in one little ring!

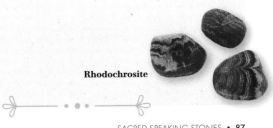

Rhodochrosite

Nature as an Altar

To dispel negative energy and overcome any blocks you feel are keeping you "stuck," go for a walk in the nearest park. Find a round, flat rock 6–10 in (15–25 cm) wide, bring it home, and clean it. Landscaping rocks and paving stones at gardening stores make marvelous outdoor altars, too. This will become an altar supplied directly to you by Mother Nature, and it will have the purest energy.

Begin by charging the stone at your home altar (see page 24) during a full moon. Ideally, you'll want to perform this spell three times during three consecutive full moons before you begin drawing upon the energy of your altar stone. Light a white candle for purification, then place your hand on the stone and chant three times:

Goddess of Night, moon of tonight,

Fill this stone with your light,

Imbue it with all your magic and might,

Surround it with your protective sight.

So mote it be. Thank you, dear Goddess.

Like your home altar, your stone or nature altar will be a reservoir to which you can turn anytime you feel stuck or uninspired. Place it in your backyard or preferred outdoor space, perhaps a deck or balcony, and turn to it when you require rejuvenation. You can also specifically invoke Persephone, a goddess of spring, by placing a pomegranate on your natural altar and adding her name as the first word of the spell given above. Make sure to thank any deity you invoke in your spell work.

Elemental Inspiration

How wonderful is it that there is a northern European goddess named Amberella whose sacred stone is none other than amber? She is an elemental deity and connected with waters, rivers, and oceans. Amber crystal is most strongly associated with creativity, inspiration, and motivation. When I am stuck in a creative slump, this is the crystal I turn to time and again to channel and attune myself to the energy of creativity, which comes from achieving flow, a state akin to the fluidity of the element of water. This simple ritual is the perfect treatment for writer's block, coming up with ideas for the next board meeting, or for facilitating progress on a forthcoming project.

Clasp the amber between your palms and feel its vibrant energy as it absorbs the warmth of your hands. Close your eyes and then claim its creative energy for yourself. Invoke the goddess Amberella:

Goddess of the waters, ancient Amberella,

I look to your springs and font of creativity.

Thanks to you, new ideas flow from me like a river.

I have cleared away any dams slowing its flow.

So mote it be and thanks to thee.

Keep the amber with you throughout the day, so it can continue to amplify the creativity you already hold inside you.

Amber

CHAPTER 5

Prosperity and
Abundance

Manifesting with the Moon

For centuries, witches have known that luck is neither random nor mysterious. Performing a spell at the optimal time in the lunar cycle will maximize your power. Thanks to the wise women in my family who shared their "trade secrets" openly, I learned very early in life that I could manifest what I wanted and needed through tools of magic and the moon. Keep this essential approach to magic in mind. When in a pinch, I have used witchcraft to replenish the coffers. I have also used prosperity spells to find a good home, attract job opportunities, and help others. Timing is everything!

Crescent Moon Magic

The crescent moon is the phase of increasing and the perfect time to lay plans for all good things you desire. Try to perform this spell when the crescent moon is waxing.

GATHER TOGETHER

pure white garment

moonstone of any size

short piece of string

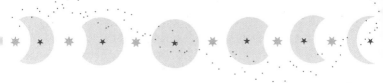

In the first quarter of the moon, don your white shirt or dress, and carry the moonstone along with you in your pocket or on a pendant. Take a late afternoon walk in a park or a meadow among wild weeds, flowers, and grasses, and gather a few as you stroll to make a bouquet. Choose a resting place and sit where you can see the crescent moon. Take your flowers and grasses and bind them with the string. Hold your newly made bouquet in your right hand. Hold your moonstone in your left hand and concentrate on your desired outcome—creative fulfillment, greater happiness, or perhaps the release of anger. Chant aloud:

Luna, in your seventh heaven, I invoke you now.

Brighter than any star, you are.

I will sing your magic song if you but show me how.

I will walk your sacred path if you but show me where.

Be here now.

Arms outspread, eyes on the moon, repeat the chant three times. As the moon shines brighter, so will your spirit.

Moonstone

Revolutionary Rocks

When choosing crystals for your altar (see page 24), select a stone that resonates with positivity. I like to switch up my touchstones frequently, but a regular go-to for me is a pretty purple amethyst. I have also used many of the revolutionary rocks mentioned opposite to good effect.

MANTRA FOR A TOUCHSTONE MEDITATION

Mantras have a special kind of manifestation power—the more you say them, the more they will come true.

If you carry a touchstone with you in a pocket, on a necklace, or tucked in a bag, you can perform this meditation anywhere, and whenever you like, because the mantra takes very little time.

Pick the calming crystal with which you have a particulate affinity and chant the below mantra aloud while holding your touchstone in both hands.

Grandmothers and Grandfathers and all the Helpers on the Other Side, I call upon you to pour forth your blessings from above.

Our planet and her people need your wisdom to be our guide. I now see your blessings raining down with more peace in the world.

I now see your blessings growing so all will be fed far and wide. I now see your blessings flowing to our Mother Earth like a tide.

May all be well, may all be loved, may all be at peace. So mote it be with gratitude unending to you on the Other Side.

KEY CRYSTALS FOR YOUR ALTAR

Amazonite

An aspirational stone of hope,
which also enhances achievement.

Apophyllite

A supportive crystal offering
encouragement and self-esteem,
which can help smooth your way
through changes.

Chrysocolla

Brings courage and will empower
you in your endeavors.

Citrine

Brings joy and keen-minded
clarity to help you envision a
brighter future.

Clear quartz

For cleansing your aura and
mindset; it will amplify your
energy and aims.

Kyanite

A letting-go stone to engender
honesty in your intentions for
yourself and toward others.

Labradorite

Like the lovely shifting colors
on its surface, this is a true stone
of transformation.

Malachite

Absorbs and removes negativity
from your surroundings and
from yourself.

Moonstone

Imparts gentle calm and provides
a strong sense of purpose and
inner strength.

Moss agate

Leads you toward your true
purpose and also away from
distraction.

Selenite

A sacred stone of peace
that can help you hone your
spiritual purpose.

Creating Your Own Wand

A wand (see page 144) is used for directing energy. It is best to make your own wand from found wood and instill it with your personal energy. It's also important to select the ideal crystal to power your tool of magic. Opposite is a guide to the magical powers inherent in different crystals so you can choose which ones to use in your spells and rituals. Abundance rites will be enhanced with bloodstone or citrine while calcite and chalcedony offer protection. See which stones work best for you.

DIRECTING YOUR DESTINY

Amethyst for balance and intuition

Aventurine for creative visualization

Bloodstone for abundance

Calcite for warding off ill fortune

Chalcedony for power over dark spirits

Citrine for motivation and success

Fluorite for contacting fairies

Garnet for protection from negativity

Hematite for strength and courage

Jade brings powerful dreams

Moss agate for powers of persuasion

Quartz crystal for divining your dreams

Rhodochrosite for seeing life's true purpose

Watermelon tourmaline for seeing the future

Amethyst

Aventurine

Bloodstone

Calcite

Chalcedony

**Watermelon
tourmaline**

A Ritual for Clarity

Quartz is the most common mineral found on the planet, and it is also excellent for putting things into perspective. Clear quartz, with its glassy sheen, can illuminate the path before you and help you better understand your desires. It will allow you to see with more clarity the circumstances that have brought you to where you are and the direction in which you are headed.

Meditate with your quartz crystal for a minute, or for as long as you like, considering what it is that you want and how you can make your desires become reality. As you meditate, this crystal will be there to guide your understanding.

Gems for Success

It is no accident that kings, queens, and emperors wore crowns. The ancients expected their leaders to be wise, and a bejeweled crown bestowed the brilliance and power of the gems on the crowned person. While you may not want to wear a tiara to the office or a crown to the grocery store, you can wear hair clips and barrettes (hairslides) with crystals and stones attached for some of the same reasons. Why not be smarter and smartly accessorized? Bejeweled barrettes worn at the temples confer wit and wisdom, a kind of brain-boosting power energy. Below are some stones to choose from.

THE CROWN JEWELS

Tiger's eye can help you filter out mental distractions; excellent for research.

Turquoise is a good stone to help keep your mind and thoughts clear.

Fluorite is a true crystal of the mind and is very good for escalating mental focus. This blue crystal helps with multitasking and managing a great deal of information.

Sodalite brings clarity and insights and combines logic and intuition—a great combo!

Abundance at Work

The world is very distracting so paying extra attention to keeping our focus goes a long way toward creating a successful working environment. Create a small shrine at home dedicated to abundance at work. It can be your home desk, a shelf, or wherever works for you.

GATHER TOGETHER

citrine or any yellow crystal or stone

1 yellow candle and 1 orange candle

benzoin incense

incense burner or fireproof dish

neroli essential oil or orange-blossom essence

bergamot essential oil

sage leaf

Arrange your shrine in a way that pleases you and stimulates your senses. Place the citrine crystal beside the yellow candle and put the benzoin—a herb for all-around mental strength and clarity—in your incense burner or fireproof dish; it will bring inspiration from the psychic realm.

Now, using the dropper in the bottle of essential oil, anoint the orange candle with the neroli oil or orange-blossom essence; then anoint the yellow candle with bergamot essential oil while you meditate to clear your mind of any distractions. This is an essential step in opening the mental and spiritual space necessary to create, whether your intention is to create a ritual of your own design or to work on an art project or a spreadsheet.

Once you feel focused, light a sage leaf and wave it around gently so the cleansing smoke permeates your shrine space. Light the anointed candles and the incense and wait a moment as the scent wafts around your newly dedicated space. Now set and speak your intention aloud:

With heart, soul, and mind,

And by the blessing of the spirits,

The fire of my focus

Burns steady and strong.

My mind is clear and sharp.

I bring my intentions into being.

The fire of my focus

Burns eternal.

Blessings to me and all who enter this space.

Let the candles and incense burn for 30 minutes before extinguishing them. Clean the incense dish and keep the candles for future rituals. Your work shrine will serve you well.

Citrine

Working Wellness

One of my good friends, Dr Helen, is a psychologist who specializes in helping people with issues around work. According to her, the number-one issue that causes panic attacks, anxiety, insomnia, and extreme stress is pressure from work and, oftentimes, overwork. The old wisdom of witchcraft can be very helpful for this thoroughly modern malady. Take matters into your own hands, literally.

Go into your backyard, a nearby meadow, or woodland and look for some loose soil. Pick up a palmful of the soil, hold it in your hands, and say aloud:

Mother of us all, I ask of you

To bring an end to what makes me blue.

No overgiving and overwork will I do.

From now on, I will stand strong and true.

Blessings to all.

Blessed be me.

Now rub the soil between your hands and meditate on feelings of peacefulness and stillness. Gently sprinkle it back to Mother Earth. Look around for small stones and take a few that appeal to your eye. When you get home, wash them and let them dry. Take at least one of the pebbles to work and place it on your desk where you see it often. It is your reminder to have healthy work habits and also to stay grounded. If worrying thoughts race into your mind, send them right back out by taking the stone into your hand and going back to the memory of when you did the grounding spell. Remember how the earth felt in your hands and how peaceful you felt. Breathe easy.

Prosperity Tree Spell

The grounded energy and rooted stability of trees makes them ideal for spellwork regarding abundance. Also, the color green is associated with wealth and most trees have an abundance of green leaves, while some even have green bark and flowers. All this makes trees perfect for conjuring cash!

GATHER TOGETHER

handful of coins, ideally very shiny new pennies, nickels, and dimes (depending on which country you are in)

small, green bowl

3 green crystals such as peridot or jade

mortar and pestle

5 large, dry maple leaves

¼ cup (50 g) granulated sugar

Place the coins in the bowl and put the crystals on top of them. To make the potion, use the mortar and pestle to grind up the maple leaves until you have about 3 teaspoons of ground leaf. Add 3 teaspoons of sugar to the ground leaves and grind well, ensuring everything is nicely combined. Then sprinkle the herbal potion on top of the coins and crystals in the bowl. Place the bowl on your altar and say aloud:

Abundance finds me and
brings bounty to me
On this day and every day.
Prosperity is on the way!
So mote it be.

Magic for True Abundance

For centuries, witches have known that luck is neither random nor mysterious. Thanks to the wise women in my family who shared their "trade secrets" openly, I learned very early in life that I could manifest my will through the tools of magic. When in a pinch, I have used witchcraft to replenish the coffers. I have also used prosperity spells to find a good home, attract job opportunities, and help others.

When I arrived penniless in San Francisco after graduate school, and realized that rent was ten times more expensive than my pocket could bear, my friends were impressed when I got a job at a prestigious stock brokerage firm on my first day job hunting, and found a spacious Victorian apartment (complete with a witchy cupola) just a few days later. None of this was accidental, I assure you.

As soon as you approach your prosperity consciously, you will see that you have the power to choose abundance. And when you increase your material prosperity, you reduce the need to worry about such worldly matters or about just getting by, day to day. Then you can move on to achieving true prosperity: expanding your mind through learning, pursuing your pleasures, spending time with family and friends, and enjoying your life.

POINTING TO PROSPERITY

For prosperity and self-improvement spells, I recommend having a wand made from ash (*Fraxinus excelsior*). Ash grows fast and its seedlings root everywhere, so it's persistent.

If your prosperity wand can fit well on your altar, I suggest keeping it there and you can also use a crystal at the end, such as citrine to boost the power of any ritual you are working on your altar. For example, whatever ritual elements symbolize money, point your wand with its crystal at those for an extra charge. See also page 96 for crystal ideas.

Money Flow

Water fountains are good feng shui and can enhance your prosperity quotient. For those of us who can't pull off a fountain in our home or garden, this works just as well to get the money flowing.

GATHER TOGETHER

at least 8 small, smooth river rocks

a large green bowl or tall vase

enough water to fill the container

your prosperity wand

Stand in the front door area of your home and identify which is the far-left corner. This is the prosperity area and, therefore, the perfect place for this ritual. Place the smooth river rocks in the bottom of the bowl or vase and carefully pour in the water so you avoid spilling any. Take up your wand and speak aloud:

In the name of the Goddess, I dedicate this space.

Peace and prosperity flows throughout this place.

Everyone here will enjoy abundance and grace.

With harm to none. So mote it be.

Gently stir the surface of the water with your wand so it swirls and circles. Repeat the spell, then bow and say thank you to the energies of abundance.

Remove the stones from the vessel and pour the water onto the roots of the nearest tree or one of your larger potted plants, ideally right outside your home. Keep the stones in the far left corner of your home for continual good feng shui. This will keep the flow of abundance in your personal space.

Prosperity Pouches

You can charge objects with magic for a specific intent by placing them on your altar for 24 hours or, for a 5-minute fix, use spellwork, as suggested here.

GATHER TOGETHER

12 in (30cm) green cord or string

1 green candle

thyme or cinnamon incense

a small muslin or cloth bag/pouch (that could fit in the palm of your hand)

bolline (see page 143)

1 cinnamon stick

1 teaspoon dried basil leaves

3 pebble-size crystals of green jade, peridot, or turquoise

Set the cord or string aside and place all the other items on your altar. Stand at your altar and light the candle and incense. Pick up the pouch and smudge it in the sweet smoke of the incense while saying the following spell:

> My life is blessed and this I know.
>
> Into this bag, prosperity will flow.
>
> I see the future is bright wherever I go,
>
> My life is blessed; this much I know.
>
> With harm to none; so mote it be.

Using your bolline, cut the cinnamon stick into 3 pieces. Cut the green cord or string into 3 pieces. Place the basil, crystals, and cinnamon into the pouch. Now take the pieces of green cord and, one at a time, tie the end of the bag securely. Keep it with you in your pocket and into your life, money will flow.

Magnetic Money Magic

Pyrite impresses every time you see it with its gleam and visual trick—it really does look like precious gold, hence its other name of "fool's gold." However, it does have the power to bring prosperity into your life. This trickster stone is associated with the mischief-maker Norse god Loki, who can be called on to attract money to you. Pyrite may not be especially valuable on its own, but its metallic golden shimmer makes it an excellent ritual tool for improving your finances.

To attract the energy of abundance and prosperity, lay the pyrite on top of something that you associate with money or success. This could be a literal wad of cash, a business card, or your savings jar, for example. Focus your intentions on what you are hoping to receive and invite this energy into your life. Loki is a messenger god, so write him a note, politely making your request. It can be as simple as: "Please bring me wealth [state here how you want this to manifest itself]." Be as specific as possible and state the amount, the timing, and so forth. Express full gratitude to Loki for his generosity, as you certainly want to stay on this mischievous god's good side! You may also carry this stone with you to work or a job interview for a little extra luck!

Coin Conjuration

We all have unexpected expenses that come out of the blue—car repairs, medical bills, or helping a loved one in need. I had the latter with my family and had to reach deep into my coffers to heed the call. When you need to recover quickly financially, this coin spell will fill the bill, literally. It is best performed Perform this spell on the evening of a new moon or during a waxing moon phase.

GATHER TOGETHER

athame (see page 143)

3 gold (or yellow) candles

frankincense or myrrh incense

3 yellow or gold-colored crystals, such as tiger's eye, amber, citrine, yellow jade, or another favorite of yours

3 pieces of yellow- or gold-colored fruit, such as yellow apples or oranges

13 coins of different denominations

a green or gold jar with a lid

Tiger's eye

Amber

Citrine

Make a quickie temporary altar (see page 24) wherever you pay your bills and handle your money—maybe it is your desk or perhaps the kitchen table. Use your athame to create the circle of magic in this soon-to-be-sacred space.

Place the candles, incense, crystals, and fruit on the temporary altar and arrange them into three groups so each group contains a crystal, piece of fruit, and candle. Light your candles and the incense. One by one, take the coins in your hand and pass them through the incense smoke. Place the coins in the jar. Now take the crystals in your hand and pass them through the smoke, then place in the jar and seal. Pick up one piece of fruit at a time and touch to your third eye (in the middle of your forehead). Pray aloud:

This offering I make as my blessing to all,

Comfort and earthly gifts upon us shall fall.

Fill my coffers with silver and gold.

In this time of great need, I will be bold.

For the good of all, young and old.

Fill my coffers with silver and gold.

And so it is.

Extinguish the candles and incense and place on your altar for future use, as well as the vessel containing the coins. When you go to sleep, dream of everyone you love, including yourself, receiving a harvest of material and spiritual wealth.

CHAPTER 6

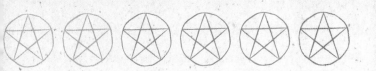

Love and Relationships

Love Magic

My very first spellwork was on the subject of love at the request of a bestie. It might have worked almost too well when they eloped after a brief courtship, but it empowered me to believe I could wield the enchanted art. It seems fitting that my dabbling in love magic came from my own love for a dear friend. What better way to start down the enchanted path than with spells for love: spells that create the potential for love, draw the attention and devotion of a lover, strengthen the union between an existing couple, invoke sexual magic, heal a broken heart, and perhaps most importantly, fill your own heart with love and compassion for yourself? Why spend a Saturday evening alone when you already know the object of your desire? No longer doubt your own power to attract, create and keep true love in your life.

Rose Quartz
for Self-Esteem

We all get worn down now and again and, when that happens, we often feel blue or at least in the doldrums a bit. If you have no other crystal, make sure to have rose quartz on hand. It infuses you with self-love and brightens the vibe anywhere it is. I view self-love as a superpower and the real foundation of all true personal power. Widely known as the stone of unconditional love, the soft pink hunk of love known as rose quartz is said to attract and inspire love in all forms. It's especially good for promoting self-love and emotional harmony. It can be a teeny tiny pebble of pink or a big ol' rock but you should have it near you, especially when you are feeling low. I say have some around at all times but, then again, I have crystals in every room. Keeping a piece of rose quartz out where we can see it, on your desk at work, on your nightstand, or next to the bathtub, can act as a powerful visual reminder to take a little bit of time for yourself.

Wanderful Love Invocation

All of us want our home to be a welcoming place for love and contentment.
You can greatly abet that outcome with this simple spell for binding love.

GATHER TOGETHER

2 pink candles

rose essential oil

2 long-stemmed pink roses

rose incense and incense burner

2 rose quartz crystals, of any size

your wand for love magic

Place all your ritual elements on a tray on your nightstand (or a chest or table
near your bed). Anoint your wand and both candles with the rose essential oil
and place the roses and the quartz crystals beside the candles. Now light the
candles and incense. Pick up your wand and intone aloud:

This is a place where joy lives.

This is a room where my heart gives.

Here is a temple to love and delight.

Here is a home filled with bliss and light.

Blessed be, and so it is.

With your wand, draw a heart shape twice in the wafting smoke of the incense,
saying "I love _____." Stand, eyes closed, while visualizing you and your partner
enjoying each other's company, happy and in love. End the ritual by saying:
"Blessed be." You can keep the tray in your bedroom as a mini shrine to love.

Your Relationship Corner

In terms of pagan feng shui, as you walk into your bedroom, the relationship corner will be at the back right. Your love and romance energies should be nurtured there, and you might consider placing a shrine there to serve as your personal wellspring to turn to when you want to refresh these feelings of felicity.

Look at this area with a fresh eye. What is cluttering your love corner with stale energy? Half-empty perfume or cosmetics bottles could be impairing your relationship energy. You must clear unhappiness out of this space by getting rid of all unnecessary objects and tidying up any clutter.

To cleanse the area, ring a handbell anywhere clutter has accumulated, giving special attention to your bed and pillows. Here are a few tips:

TIPS FOR A HAPPY HOMESTEAD

Never bring old pillows into a new home. These can cause poor sleep and bad dreams, carry old sexual energy, and kill a relationship.

•

Never place your bed in the center of the room. This will cause anxiety and get in the way of a healthy relationship.

•

Never place the bed so that its foot (the bottom of the bed) faces the door, as this brings very bad luck.

•

To keep your romantic life fresh, make the bed every morning and change the linens often.

Loved-One Shrine

This sacred space is dedicated to the special people in your life: friends, family, and your partner. Your shrine can be a low table or even a shelf and provides a place to put gifts you have received from your loved ones, which might include crystals, jewelry, art, and lovely objects along with all their photos in frames. Every time I see my own special Loved-one Shrine, I smile. It fills my heart with love.

GATHER TOGETHER

sage for smudging

a pink cloth or scarf

2 pink candles and 2 white candles

a small rose quartz and fluorite crystals

a vase of fresh cut flowers of your choice (daisies, for example)

To set up your shrine, purify the space by lighting the sage bundle and letting the smoke waft around the area. This is called "smudging" and is an essential part of witchcraft. You can use wild sage or purchase it in any herb store. Once you have smudged the space, cover your sacred space with the scarf or cloth, and place the candles in each of the four corners. (Pink is the color of affection and white represents purity.) Place the crystals around the vase of fresh flowers—whichever ones connote fun and friendship to you. Then add gifts or other trinkets that remind you of your loved one.

Light the candles, kneel before your newly created shine and say the words opposite:

I light the fire of loyalty

The heat of heart and the flame of love and friendship.

Brightest blessing, Great Goddess bring,

The spirit of friendship will surely sing.

As the fates do dance, I welcome the chance

To share my love and my life.

So mote it be.

THE FLAME OF FRIENDSHIP

You can further charge the candles on your Loved-one Shrine by scratching your desire into the wax. I use the thorn of a rose for this and write the words of my intention. Many witches use symbols: a moon, the sun, a flower, a heart, a dollar sign, or a number, for example. You can also inscribe a name.

Take a large solar-hued yellow pillar candle anointed with lemon or bergamot essential oil and charge it with positivity toward your loved ones. Scratch your own name into it and write "I love _____" with the name of your friend or family member.

Light the candle and say four times:

I love me. I love _____.

For a daily dose of one-minute magic, light the candle every night and repeat this love charge before bed and every morning when you arise. Your heart will lift and soar, which then emanates outward toward this special person in your life.

Twin-Hearts Love Spell

If you are seeking a soul mate, this simple spell will do the trick.

Perform this spell on the next new moon. Take two pieces of heart-shaped rose quartz and stand in the center of your bedroom. Light two pink candles and recite these words:

Beautiful crystal I hold this night,

Flame with love for my delight.

Harm to none as love comes to me.

This I ask and so shall it be.

Keep the candles and crystals on your bedside table and think of it as a shrine to love. Repeat three nights in a row and ready yourself for *amour*.

Blissings Box for Self-Love

Altars are perfect places to keep treasure boxes of ceremonial incenses and other sacred tools. In the following ritual crystals, herbs, and flowers remind you to hold yourself in the highest esteem. Scent is such a powerful signal to the brain and every time you need a lift, you can open this box of bliss and breathe in pure love.

GATHER TOGETHER

¼ cup (5 g) pink rose petals

¼ cup (10 g) dried lavender

¼ cup (10 g) dried oregano

small mixing bowl

3 drops lavender essential oil

3 drops rose essential oil

small wooden box with lid

pink jade, red jade, or rose quartz crystal

Try to perform this rite during a new moon. Place the flower petals and herbs into the bowl and gently mix together. Add the essential oils and mix again, then fill the box with the herbal mix. Settle the crystal in the herbs right at the top, then close the lid and place the box on your altar. Each night, open the box up and breathe in the lovely fragrance that will envelope you in an aura of love.

Amber's Emotional Healing Power

In Norse mythology, amber comes from the goddess Freya's tears that fell into the sea when she wandered the earth weeping and looking for her husband, Odin. Those tears that fell on dry land turned into golden amber. Now amber is believed to be very helpful and comforting to those who are separated and/or getting divorced, especially women, and to anyone who is experiencing grief.

Jade Rainbow Ritual

If you are hurting, in this heart-healing ritual choose jade of the color that suits your need best (see opposite) and say:

My heart is heavy and hurting,

I ask the universe for relief.

Harm to none but release for me,

I long to heal and be free,

And so it is.

COLORS OF JADE

Purple jade heals a broken heart, allowing understanding and acceptance in and pain and anger out. If you are going through a breakup, purple jade will help you with the heartache.

Green jade is the counselor stone and can help a relationship that isn't working to become functional instead of dysfunctional. This shade is also a boon for the brain. Green jade helps with getting along.

Red jade promotes the proper release of anger and also generates sexual passion. Serve your lover a passion potion in a cup of carved red jade while wearing only red jade. Sparks will fly!

Blue jade is a rock for patience and composure and for conveying a sense of control. Wear blue jade pendants for serenity.

Yellow jade is for energy, simple joy, and maintaining a sense of being a part of a greater whole. A yellow jade bracelet or ring will help you to feel that all is well in your world.

Freya's Love Beads
Meditation

Freya is a many-faceted goddess: mother, protector, wife, lover, and healer, but she is akin to Venus, the goddess of love, in many ways. A string of rose quartz prayer beads can imbue your life with romance and essential self-love. This lovely pink mineral is the stone of unconditional love and will instantly attract love from yourself and others. Rose quartz will open your heart to giving and receiving the bounties of love—self-love, familial love, romantic love, or whatever it is that you wish to manifest in your life. It can be used in a short string of a dozen beads or even as a bracelet.

Take your rose quartz string of beads and rest it against your heart as you meditate for just a few minutes on its properties and the love that you want to give and receive. Close your eyes and speak loving words and affirmations to yourself or repeat an incantation such as this: "Loving kindness flows from me. Love to myself, and love to all. So mote it be." The words can vary depending on your intentions. Let the loving energy of the rose quartz fill you and embolden you to love wildly and fearlessly.

True Love Magic

For this love spell use cherry fruit and rose quartz stones to bring lasting love into your life.

GATHER TOGETHER
square of pink cloth, 9 x 9 in (23 x 23 cm)

pen with red ink

9 cherries

2 rose quartz stones

small red dish

Fill your mind with thoughts of love and visualize your prospective partner. On one side of the piece of cloth, in the center, draw two large overlapping hearts in red ink. Pick up two cherries. Place them in the center of the hearts and say, "This represents true and mutual love." Pick up two more cherries and say, "This represents a loving and equal exchange." Pick up two more and say, "These two for truth and loyalty." Pick up two more and say, "These stand for the bloom of good health and endurance." Pick up the last cherry and say, "This sweet fruit stands for the everlasting bond that unites us. May it stay strong for all eternity." Take the rose quartz stones, place them with the cherries, and say, "May this love stand the test of time and be set for all eternity... and so it is."

Now eat the cherries and put the pits (stones), which are the cherry seeds, in the red dish, then place this in your bedroom along with the two rose quartz stones and the cloth for at least nine days. All the while, the seeds will be emanating the energy of the true love coming your way.

Crystal Cave Consecration

Even when you don't have your crystals with you, you can harness their power through powerful visualizations, such as this one. Find a quiet place where you won't be interrupted to perform the following meditation. You may wish to record it so you can listen to it with closed eyes.

Blessed beings, you are about to enter the Crystal Cave of our great Mother Earth, Gaia. In your mind, you are standing with bare feet on the ground. You can feel the grass with your toes, the solid earth underneath your feet. Feel the solidity and fastness of the earth fill your body with strength; we are all made of earth, of clay. We come from the earth and we are made of earth. Feel your connection to the Mother. We come from the earth, her womb. We are made of stardust, clay, and the waters of the ocean. Feel the blood in your veins, the water of life. Know that you are alive. Feel her winds, the breath of life. Breathe deeply ten times, completely filling your lungs and completely emptying your lungs. Breathe and feel your chest expand, rising and falling with each breath.

Now feel your backbone connecting to the earth; you feel a silver cord connecting you and your life to the earth. Concentrate on the cord until you can feel it running all the way through you and deep into the earth. Tug on the cord; feel it give. Now, take the cord in your hands and follow it down, down, deep into the earth. It is dark as you go down and down, but you are not at all frightened, as you are a denizen of the dark. Trust in the universe and keep descending into the bosom of the Mother. Down we go, not falling, but moving purposefully, gracefully, following the cord into the earth. Now you can see light. Keep moving toward the light and keep holding the cord as it leads you to the shining distance.

The light grows nearer, and you see that it is an opening—a cave, a safe place for shelter. Enter the cave. It is filled with firelight reflecting off a thousand crystal points. A lovely and mysterious older woman sits near the fire, warming her bones in her comfortable and dry cave. She is bestrewn with jewels and is dressed in a velvet and gossamer robe that is iridescent and shines in the firelight. Her visage is that of an incredibly wise woman, and you can simply tell she has the knowledge of all time and the history of the world.

The cave is beautiful, more beautiful than the palace of any king or queen. It is the Crystal Cave of the Goddess, and you are with her. Show your respect to the Goddess and light the incense at her altar at the side of the cave, which has piles of many shimmering stones and priceless gems, the bounty and beauty of our generous benefactor. Sit at her feet and take in her love, power, and grace. Sit quietly and hear the special message she has for you. You are her child, and she has dreamed a dream for you. When you have received your Goddess-gifted message, let the cord guide you back to the surface. Release the cord and bow in gratitude to the Great Goddess.

CHAPTER 7

Divination and Psychic Vision

Prompt Prophecies

Give your tarot cards a rest and create a one-of-a-kind divination tool:
a bag of crystals you can use to do readings. I have used this divination tool
for matters ranging from career, wealth, health, love, and travel.

Select a favorite velvet bag, and fill it with a selection of crystals. Ideally you
should include all the stones listed opposite, but if you cannot, you should have
at least a dozen to start with (see below).

Casting the stones is as easy as one, two, three:

1. Shake the bag well.

2. Ask a question.

3. Remove the first three stones you touch, and then interpret them
using the guide opposite.

COLLECTING CRYSTALS

Most of us cannot afford diamonds in our bag of crystals, so substitute
with clear quartz; for emeralds, switch to peridots, and garnets can
substitute nicely for rubies. Some New Age stores and online sources
have "rough rubies" and "rough emerald" pieces for just a few dollars
each, so it is possible to find these spiritual stones at reasonable prices.
You can also usually acquire relatively inexpensive stones, such as
garnets, agates, amethysts, and tiny citrines, at your favorite metaphysical
shop or you can buy them online.

CRYSTAL MEANINGS

Amethyst: change is coming

Aventurine: new horizons and positive growth

Black agate: monetary gain

Blue lace agate: the need for spiritual and physical healing

Citrine: the universe offers enlightenment

Diamond: stability

Emerald: lushness

Hematite: new prospects

Jade: everlasting life

Lapis lazuli: heavenly fortune

Quartz: clarity where there was none

Red agate: long life and health

Red jasper: the need for grounding

Rose quartz: love is in your life

Ruby: deep passion and personal power

Sapphire: truth

Snowflake obsidian: your troubles are at an end

Snow quartz: major changes

Tiger's eye: the situation is not as it appears

Snow quartz

Snowflake obsidian

Activate Your Third Eye

Labradorite is a stunning stone. When cut and polished, it is fascinating, with an impressive light show of yellows, oranges, blues, and violets. The special play of light and color across the surface is called labradorescence. The effect is caused by lamellar intergrowths, produced inside the crystal while the crystal formed. Named after the place it was first found, Labrador, this crystal can also be found in India, Finland, Russia, Newfoundland, and Madagascar.

This bluish feldspar is a soul stone with a very powerful light energy. It abets astral travel and connecting with the higher consciousness. It brings up nothing but positivity for the mind and excises the lower energies of anxiety, stress, and negative thoughts. It is an aura cleanser and balancer. Labradorite also protects against aura leakage wherein your personal energy drains out, leading to mental exhaustion and a case of the blues.

I had no idea that it is also a stone that awakens psychic powers and activates your third eye until I learned this from the great teacher Scott Cunningham. Even a small piece of this special crystal will work. Take the crystal and hold it to the center of your forehead with both hands. Speak aloud:

Artemis, Astarte, Athena, Circe—fill me with your power,

On this day, I ask you lend me your seer's vision.

I stand at the threshold in this holy hour.

And so it is. Great goddesses; I am grateful.

Labradorite

Astral Azurite Spell

The great psychic and healer Edgar Cayce used this blue beauty for achieving remarkable meditative states during which he had astoundingly accurate visions and prophetic dreams. Indeed, azurite helps achieve a high state of mental clarity and powers of concentration. If you cannot find the answer to a problem in the here and now, try looking for solutions on the astral plane.

First, write the problem down on paper and place it under a small azurite overnight on a windowsill so it collects moonlight.

The next day at 11:11 a.m., lie comfortably in a quiet and darkened room with the azurite stone placed over your third eye (between your eyebrows) on your forehead. Clear your mind of everything for 11 minutes and meditate. Sit up and listen for the first thing that comes into your mind—it should be the answer or a message regarding the issue at hand. Write down the words you receive. The rest of the day you will be in a state of grace and higher mind, during which you will hear information and answers to help guide you in many aspects of your life.

If, like me, you enjoy this meditation, you may want to do it every day at 11:11 a.m. and every night at 11:11 p.m. I strongly suggest that you keep a journal of these "azurite answers." You may receive information that you will not understand until many years have passed, making the journal an invaluable resource and key to your very special life.

Divination Moonstone

Moonstone is reputed to be the most powerful crystal for use in rune stones, the tools used for a specialized form of divination. Runes, or letters from a language used by early Nordic peoples, are carved into the stones and are said to hone and intensify the intuition of the reader divining the future from them. You, too, can use a bag of lustrous and mysterious small moonstones to get in touch with your powers of perception. While others throw the I Ching or read their horoscopes with their morning coffee, you can take out a moonstone, look at the pattern carved in its beautifully reflective surface, and contemplate its meaning for your day.

MOONSTONE MIRROR RITE

If you are feeling out-of-sorts or off-center, turn to this lovely stone, which is sacred to the shining orb in the night sky. Gaze at the moon on a moonlit night, then at your smooth, round moonstone, and look for the answer to your personal mystery. A message will come to you in the form of a dream that night.

Scrying Stones

The great seers can use a mirror, a still surface of water, or any reflective surface for prophetic purpose. Any polished stone can serve the same purpose. Here are some marvelous crystals for divination. Sit in a darkened room, hold the smooth stone in your hand, and gaze at it. It may take a few moments but you will begin to see flickering and even images on the surface. What you see are messages specifically for you.

MYSTIC HELPERS

Amethyst opens your psychic abilities.

Azurite with malachite can help you to conceive new ideas.

Bloodstone guards you against deceit from others.

Celestite gives you the very special help of angel-powered insight and advice.

Chrysocolla helps you to foresee difficulties, including romantic ones.

Lapis lazuli leads the way for the new in your life.

Selenite can be used under moonlight for visions of your ideal future.

Celestite

Become a Stone Seer

Crystals are an excellent tool for divination. If you are expecting a direct answer to your questions from divining with crystals, you may be dissatisfied, but they are wonderful when you are stuck in a sticky situation and seeking to gain clarity regarding your quandary! Keep your mind and heart open and try this dazzling divination method for yourself.

The first step in this divination practice is to procure a bag for your crystals. This bag can be something meaningful for you, but it could also be any repurposed container that will hide the crystals from view. I recommend using something that is pleasing to your eye, such as a silken satchel or velvety drawstring pouch—perhaps even one made of a selenite-infused fabric—purchased from your local metaphysical store. Once you have placed your crystals inside the bag, you are ready to begin.

Take out a single crystal. You need to make a mental note of its color, or jot this down on a piece of paper. Put the crystal back in the bag, and then draw out a second crystal. Again, write down the color and then put the crystal back in the bag. Repeat this process one more time until you have retrieved a total of three crystals.

First crystal: The first of the three crystals is indicative of the issue at hand. It may draw your attention to an existing problem, or perhaps bring to the surface an underlying matter that you may not have been consciously aware of.

Second crystal: This crystal is antagonistic and represents something that may be preventing you from reaching a solution.

Third crystal: The final crystal shows where you will find your solution—the key to regaining your peace of mind!

ANSWERS TO YOUR TROUBLES

Here are some examples of the issues and answers that the various crystals might point you toward:

Red stones (garnet, ruby, jasper, jade, bloodstone)

First stone: You might be feeling frustrated about something that is occurring in your life.

Second stone: There are likely many strong emotions involved in the issue at hand, which may be a source of hostility.

Third stone: You will find a solution to your troubles by transforming negative emotions from yourself or other involved individuals into something more constructive; translate anger into affirmative action rather than letting it simmer.

Pink stones (topaz, rose quartz, rhodochrosite)

First stone: Perhaps your conflict lies in the divide between following your heart, and pursuing what is right for you, and doing what is best for the world at large.

Second stone: Your own sense of self- importance and your material desires are distracting you.

Third stone: Treat everyone you meet with love as though they are dear to your heart, even if they are strangers to you.

Purple stones (amethyst, fluorite, lepidolite)

First stone: There may be some disruption in your life caused by an imbalance between your earthly life and your spirituality.

Second stone: You are letting minor concerns and trials divert your attention from what truly matters to you.

Third stone: When difficulties come your way, take them in your stride. Allow a sense of calm to fill you as you remember that your struggles will pass and be forgotten in light of the grander scheme of things.

Continued overleaf

Blue stones (aquamarine, lapis lazuli, sapphire)

First stone: You may be facing a dilemma as to whether you should say what's on your mind or leave things to chance.

Second stone: The people in your life will take advantage of you if you do not stand up for yourself or make your voice heard. Your quiet will become their permission.

Third stone: Be honest and speak without fear. When the truth comes out, justice will take its due course.

Green stones (malachite, jade, aventurine)

First stone: Perhaps you are facing a situation where you need to decide whether to follow the whims and longings of your heart or sacrifice your own wellbeing for the sake of someone else.

Second stone: There is a possibility that your loving soul has put you in a position to be used by others who would emotionally manipulate you for their own purposes.

Third stone: Listen to what your instinct tells you. You need to trust yourself more, and give of yourself only if it feels right, not because of any outside influence. You will know what the right choice is.

Yellow stones (citrine, jasper, honey calcite)

First stone: You are trying to be in too many places and do too many things at once.

Second stone: Though you may put time and dedication into what you do, your endeavors are being sabotaged. At the root of the problem lies deceit and envy.

Third stone: Be mindful of the things that the people in your life have to say about you. Some of them may be more accurate than you care to admit, regardless of whether those things are positive or negative. Keep your priorities in order.

Orange stones (sunstone, amber, carnelian)

First stone: You may find that your emotional needs are being neglected. Alternatively, there is a chance that you are not staying true to yourself and what you believe in some facet of your life.

Second stone: There may be someone overstepping their boundaries and exerting their influence and control over you. You may be blissfully unaware of this, especially if that person is being subtle in the way they've been overshadowing you.

Third stone: Be kind and firm as you enforce your boundaries. You need to stand up for yourself and what you deserve, but this does not need to be at the expense of anyone else's self-image.

Black stones (obsidian, tourmaline, onyx)

First stone: You have quite a few affairs in your life that have been left unsettled.

Second stone: You are trapped in a position that is detrimental to you, but your own worries and insecurities are keeping you there.

Third stone: The best way to solve your dilemma is by using acts of kindness and love to negate harmful energies and destructive frames of mind.

White stones (moonstone, howlite, selenite)

First stone: It's possible that you are feeling discontented with the way you are living and want to make some sort of significant change.

Second stone: The idea of change makes you anxious as it may threaten to upset the lifestyle you've grown comfortable with.

Third stone: Now is the time to set changes in motion. Be gentle with yourself as you transition into new experiences and phases of life and release your fear of the unknown.

Gray stones (smoky quartz, labradorite, moonstone)

First stone: You're stuck in a liminal space between clinging to the past and moving on.

Second stone: It may be that uncertainty is preventing you from realizing your potential. Doubt on your part or that of someone closely involved in your life is becoming too pervasive.

Third stone: Find resolution in knowing that nothing in life is ever truly black and white, and this includes the issues that trouble you. The gray space in between is what gives you the freedom to make your own way.

Crystal Ball Vision

When selecting a crystal ball, your choice should not be taken lightly. This is a very personal tool that will become instilled with your energy. Crystal balls have their own authority and they can strongly influence the development of our psychic abilities.

You should think of the crystal as a container that houses your energy, so make sure it feels right for you. The crystal should feel comfortable to hold—not too heavy and not too light. You should not allow anyone else to touch your crystal ball. If someone does touch it, place the ball in a bowl of sea salt overnight to cleanse it of outside energy and influence. Quartz crystal balls have inherent power, so you have to practice working with them first. Pure quartz crystal balls can be quite expensive, but the price is worth it if you are serious about harnessing your intuition and using it for good. And don't expect your experiences to be like the movies! Most of the people I know who use crystal balls, including many healers and teachers, see cloudy and smoky images.

Work with a partner to sharpen your psychic skills. Sit directly across from your partner with the crystal ball between you. Close your eyes halfway and look at the ball and into the ball while harnessing your entire mind. Empty out all other thoughts and focus as hard as you can. You will sense your third eye, the traditional seat of psychic awareness, begin to open and project into the crystal ball. By practicing this way, you will train your mind. The patterns you see will become clearer and your impressions more definite. You should trust that what you are seeing is real and find a place of knowing. For me, my gut seems to be an additional center of intuition. I just "know in my gut" when something is amiss. Verbalize to your partner what you see, and then listen to your partner as they reveal their visions to you.

You should also do crystal ball meditations on your own. In a darkened room, sit and hold your crystal ball in the palms of both hands. Touch it to your heart and then gently touch it to the center of your forehead, where your third eye is located. Then hold the ball in front of your physical eyes and, sitting very still, gaze into it for at least 3 minutes. Envision pure white light in the ball and hold on to that image. Practice the white-light visualization for up to a half hour and then rest your mind, your eyes, and your crystal ball. If you do this every day, within a month you should start to become adept at crystal-ball gazing.

When we gaze into a crystal ball, it is possible to see into the fabric of time, both the past and the future. At first you may be able to see a flickering, wispy, suggestive image. Some of you may be able to see clearly defined visions on your first try. Most of us have to practice and hone our attunement to the energy of the ball. You must clearly establish your interpretation of what you see. Many psychics use a crystal ball in their readings, and some report seeing images of clients' auras in the ball. Projecting information about people's lives is a huge responsibility, so you need to feel sure about what you are reading. Learn to trust your body's center of intuition.

Divining a Brighter Future

Nothing is more vital than the breath, which is the source of all energy. It behooves everyone who uses a crystal ball to learn to control the breath. All professional seers, like all professional clairvoyants, cultivate deep breathing, for they are aware that their psychic powers are enhanced by their lung capacity. Deep breathing is a great aid to concentration, just as physical ease helps to erase irritability and ensure a patient attitude.

Three periods during the day are ideal times to consult the crystal ball: sunrise, midday, and sunset, although this does not preclude other hours between dawn and dusk. It is generally accepted that sunrise is the most propitious, for it symbolizes a new beginning. Times to avoid using the crystal ball are the dark hours from nine o'clock in the evening until dawn. During that period the scryer is renewing vital powers, either through sleep or meditation.

As a crystal-ball seer, you will notice clouding in your crystal, which may appear in various forms: as a milky obscurity, as a smoky, impenetrable mist, or as minuscule white clouds drifting through the crystal ball. White clouds are an affirmative indication of coming favors. If brilliance breaks through the clouds, it is indicative of the sun, which will light the way to better financial circumstances and to improved physical health. However, if a soft light lacking brilliance appears through the clouds, it is indicative of the moon, which foretells a period of inaction that may be likened to the recuperation of the vital forces.

CRYSTAL BALL MEANINGS

Black: When the cloud is black, that is the time to be concerned, for a black cloud is unfavorable, even ill-omened. The seriousness of the prediction is measured by the degree of blackness. Does the blackness appear in a small portion of the crystal ball, or does it fill the entire globe?

Color: Occasionally, the clouds take on a show of color. When clouds of red, orange, or yellow appear, the portents are ominous. Red clouds foretell dangerous situations—accidents, serious illness, and grief. Orange clouds predict loss of material goods and friendship. Yellow clouds bring deception and ultimate betrayal by supposed friends.

Green, blue, or violet: If green, blue, or violet suffuse the crystal ball, this is an excellent indication. When green clouds appear, the individual will be called on to assist as a neighborhood mediator in an educational, political, or religious capacity. If a blue cloud appears, an occasion will arise that requires shrewd discernment and which will bring both honor and praise to the individual. When a violet cloud floats through the crystal ball, a latent talent may be recognized, or a worthy philosophical expression will be presented and well received.

Gifts from Nature

Stones, crystals, and gems are regarded as the purest forms of the earth's generosity. Whenever you get a new crystal or a piece of jewelry with a stone or gem or decorate your home or garden with rocks and pebbles, show gratitude for these gifts from nature. This spell combines the power of crystals and that of thankfulness, which has been proven scientifically to improve mental health by Dr Robert Emmons in a study at University of California.

GATHER TOGETHER

⅓ cup (¼ oz/5 g) thyme

½ cup (¼ oz/5 g) daisies

⅓ cup (1 oz/30 g) ground cinnamon

1 stick of cinnamon incense

Sprinkle the daisy blossoms, thyme, and ground cinnamon on your garden path and on your doorstep. Push the incense stick into the ground by the path and light it. Stand on the threshold of your door and chant aloud:

Mother Nature, I thank you for the strength

And bounty of your stones and bones.

Your beauty is reflected now and forever.

Blessed be all, Blessed be thee.

Leave the flowers, herbs, and spice on the path—every time you step on them, you are activating blessings. Your gratitude will be rewarded tenfold, and you will enjoy a shower of crystals and gems in your life from Mother Nature, who enjoys getting credit for her good works!

GLOSSARY OF TERMS

Altar

"Raised structure or place used for worship or prayer" upon which a Wiccan practitioner places several symbolic and functional items for the purpose of worshiping the God and Goddess, casting spells, and/or saying chants and prayers.

Athame

An athame (pronounced "a-THAW-may") is used to direct the energies raised in your ritual. Since black is the color that absorbs energy, athames should have a dark handle as well as a dull blade, and be placed on the right side of your altar.

Besom

A tool used in Wicca to cleanse and purify a space to be used for ritual; also referred to as a broom.

Bolline

A bolline is a white-handled knife that is used for making other tools and for cutting materials, such as cords and herbs, in your magical workings.

Book of Shadows

A journal in which to keep a record of your magical work. It should also be a book of inspiration for you, filled with your own thoughts, personal poetry, and observations; most helpful if you use it daily or as often as possible.

Candles

Represent earth, fire, air, and water. Different colors conjure different enchantments. You can "dress" or anoint the side of the candle with a couple of drops of essential oil using a dropper or cotton ball.

Essential oils

Distillations of herbs and flowers, ideally organic. When you are making a blend of oils or a potion or lotion, mix them with a carrier (or base) oil, such as jojoba, almond, apricot, grapeseed, or sesame, to dilute the essential oil and make it safe to apply to the skin. Always test a blend on a small area of the skin first and leave for 24 hours to check you don't have any reaction to it.

Incense

Powdered herbs, roots, and resins to burn on your altar or in your spells to further your intention. Most New-Age, herb, and health-food stores have a wide variety of cone, stick, and loose incense. Use a sensor or glass dish for burning incense safely.

Smudging

The burning of bundles of sage or other dried herbs to purify and clear a space. Sage bundles are readily available at any New-Age store and are essential to keep on hand for much of your ritual work. You can dry your own herbs for bundling and burning in a fireproof dish.

Wand

Rods, ideally made from fallen tree branches, which are used to direct magical workings; instruments used by witches and magicians in spellwork and ritual.

PICTURE CREDITS